THE
DOUBLE SORROW
OF TROILUS

A Study of Ambiguities in
Troilus and Criseyde

BY

IDA L. GORDON

The double sorwe of Troilus to tellen,
That was the kyng Priamus sone of Troye,
In lovynge how his aventures fellen
Fro wo to wele, and after out of joie,
My purpos is, or that I parte fro ye.

OXFORD
AT THE CLARENDON PRESS
1970

Oxford University Press, Ely House, London W. 1

GLASGOW NEW YORK TORONTO MELBOURNE WELLINGTON
CAPE TOWN SALISBURY IBADAN NAIROBI DAR ES SALAAM LUSAKA ADDIS ABABA
BOMBAY CALCUTTA MADRAS KARACHI LAHORE DACCA
KUALA LUMPUR SINGAPORE HONG KONG TOKYO

PR1896
G6

PRINTED IN GREAT BRITAIN
AT THE UNIVERSITY PRESS, OXFORD
BY VIVIAN RIDLER
PRINTER TO THE UNIVERSITY

Preface

THE writing of this book was made easier by a sabbatical year, for which I must thank the Vice-Chancellor and Council of Manchester University, but it is really the outcome of many years' teaching, which has forced me to the close verbal analysis that Chaucer's poetry demands, and all too often does not get, and which has sent me, for help, to the works of Chaucerian scholars and medievalists notably in the fields of philosophy and literary history. I am grateful to all these writers, and their publishers, and most of all to those whose contribution to this book is acknowledged within its pages. The commentary on *Troilus and Criseyde* is now so vast that I find it difficult to make a selection beyond this; and for this reason, and because bibliographies of all Chaucer's poems are readily accessible, I have not included a bibliography here.

I am grateful also to Dr. D. P. Henry, of the Philosophy Department of Manchester University, for reading and correcting the first draft of my chapter on Boethius—if there are errors in the final version, the responsibility is mine—and to Professor Eugène Vinaver, who has encouraged and stimulated me in my work, both directly and through his medieval seminar for members of staff.

Finally, I wish to thank Mr. D. M. Davin, of the Clarendon Press, for his help and advice during the preparation of the book for publication.

Contents

viiiContents

Book II, Lines 1–49
Book III, Lines 1394–1413
Book II, Lines 666–79
Shorter Interventions in Books III, IV, V
Book V, Lines 1786–99

IV. AMBIGUITY AND THE NARRATIVE   93
The Love Imagery
Antigone's Song
The Characterization of Criseyde
The Complementary roles of Troilus and
    Pandarus
Troilus of Book IV and the Reason/Desire
    Conflict
Troilus and Diomede
Pandarus

V. CONCLUSION AND SUMMARY   130
Irony and Emotional Effect
Troilus' Address to Criseyde's Empty House
The Nature of the Allegory
Summary of the Morality

APPENDIX. *Kynde* and *Unkynde*   145

LIST OF REFERENCES TO *TROILUS AND
    CRISEYDE*   151

INDEX   153

Abbreviations

ELH   *A Journal of English Literary History*
MLN   *Modern Language Notes*
MLQ   *Modern Language Quarterly*
MLR   *Modern Language Review*
MP   *Modern Philology*
OED   *Oxford English Dictionary*
PMLA   *Publications of the Modern Language Association of America*
SP   *Studies in Philology*

CHAPTER I

Introductory

The Problem of Ambiguity

W ILLIAM E MPSON writes at the beginning of his
Seven Types of Ambiguity:

> An ambiguity, in ordinary speech, means something very
> pronounced, and as a rule witty or deceitful. I propose to
> use the word in an extended sense, and shall think relevant
> to my subject any verbal nuance, however slight, which gives
> room for alternative reactions to the same piece of language.[1]

For him the distinction was necessary, since he often
discusses as ambiguities 'pieces of language' that would not
ordinarily be considered ambiguous. For me it would be a
dangerous distinction, since the ambiguities I shall be
discussing, however slight their verbal nuances, must be
witty or deceitful in some degree, if the ambiguity is part
of the total effect intended. A convenient example offers
itself in the last of the passages that Empson himself chooses
from Chaucer's *Troilus and Criseyde* to illustrate his second
type of ambiguity ('where two or more meanings are
resolved into one'). It is a stanza from the scene where
Criseyde has yielded to the persuasion of Pandarus so far
as to admit Troilus into her bedroom; it is spoken by the
narrator, and reads, in Empson's version:

> But now pray God to quenchen al this sorwe.
> So hope I that he shall, for he best may.

[1] p. 1 in the 2nd edn. (Penguin Books in assoc. with Chatto & Windus,
1965).

> For I have seen of a full misty morwe
> Folwe ful ofte a merie somer's day
> And after winter folweth grene May.
> Men sen alday, and reden eke in stories,
> That after sharpe shoures ben victories.

The ambiguity that Empson finds is in *shoures*:

> It meant charge, or onslaught of battle, or pang, such as Troilus' fainting-fits, or the pains of childbirth; if you take it as showers of rain . . . the two metaphors, from man and the sky, melt into each other; there is another connection with warriors, in that the word is used for showers of arrows; there is another connection with lovers in that it is used for showers of tears.[1]

This analysis, the more flighty bits apart, does something to explain the poetic effect of this passage—but not perhaps enough. Empson had described it as a 'sheer song of ironical happiness', and it would be interesting to know just what made him feel this particular passage to be ironical—how far it was just an assumption from his own understanding of the poem, or how far there is something specific in the passage itself to suggest irony. Is there an ironic ambiguity in the word 'victories'? The melting into each other of the metaphors lends to the idea of victory the beauty that belongs to the concept of May coming after winter and a fine summer's day following a misty morning, but if we remember that 'victory' includes the success of Pandarus' trick, we must be aware simultaneously of the beauty and the dubiousness of its application here. But unless the ambiguity was intended it is really irrelevant—and this is where the problem lies.

Troilus and Criseyde is full of verbal nuances which give room for alternative reactions in this way: it is the cumulation of them that has made possible the variant interpreta-

[1] p. 67.

tions of the poem, since it is left to the reader to decide whether, or in what ways, the ambiguity is part of the total effect intended. And his reaction depends in large measure on the initial assumptions with which he approaches the poem. The reader with little or no knowledge of its genesis, its medieval background, may well fail to find any but the most obvious ambiguities—such readers have tended to regard the Christian 'moralitee' of the epilogue as a concession to the times, something that sits more or less uneasily on an otherwise commendably 'modern' love story. At the other end of the scale is the scholarly critic who proceeds on the assumption that the only way to look at the poem is through what history can tell us that is relevant to it. But though history (to quote Charles Muscatine) 'gives us signposts to the probable areas of relevance . . . helps to prevent gross errors of analysis, such as those that proceed from reading a work by the wrong set of assumptions',[1] it cannot in itself interpret the work for us. If it could, scholastic research might have led progressively towards agreement about the interpretation of *Troilus and Criseyde*; and it has not done so. This is partly because each scholar tends to explore a particular historical field, and to interpret the poem in the light of his findings. In this way history, while illuminating, tends to distort, and so itself becomes one of the sources of variant interpretation. But there are more important reasons why history can never in itself reveal the meaning of the poem, and does not even necessarily prevent errors of analysis. A good poet, working in a well-established tradition, usually assimilates to his own individual ends both the solutions that the tradition provides and contemporary attitudes to them, using both critically.

[1] *Chaucer and the French Tradition* (Univ. of California Press, 1964), p. 4.

The peculiar significance of his work may derive neither exactly from within the tradition, nor from a breaking away from it, but from finding in it greater potentialities, or problems, than had been realized before. For the critic, the genetic approach helps to establish the nature, weight, and relevance of the traditional ideas or topics, and the function of the traditional modes of expression, but it cannot determine what those ideas meant to the poet, or what the tools of expression can be made to do in his hands. For example, as Robert Payne has shown so ably,[1] an understanding of the medieval theories of poetry can help towards a greater appreciation of Chaucer's methods in this poem, but those theories are sometimes applied by him to effects the theorists might not have foreseen. In the same way, while medieval philosophical doctrine can point the way to 'the probable areas of relevance' of the poem, the more alive we are to those probable areas of relevance the more demands the poem seems to make on our own critical responses. One of the gains of recent criticism has been to make clearer the relevance of the epilogue to the narrative: it has not gone so far as to enable critics to reach agreement about the attitude the poet is asking us to take to his story and persons. On the one hand, for example, is Charles Muscatine's view that the irony of the narrative lies in its manipulation of 'two equally admirable, equally incomplete attitudes to life' (the 'courtly' and the 'practical'); this view sees the morality in terms of 'the imperfection inherent in any mode of life—be it practical or idealistic—wherein the end itself is *earthly* joy, and hence wherein the prize may at any moment be washed away by the same tides that brought it in.'[2] On the other hand is D. W. Robertson's

---

[1] *The Key of Remembrance: A Study of Chaucer's Poetics* (Yale Univ. Press, 1963).   [2] *Chaucer and the French Tradition*, p. 132.

view of the narrative as a medieval allegory, in which
the love story is an ironical depiction of *cupiditas*.[1] Each
sees the morality of the epilogue to be inherent in the narrative (and a story designed to illustrate the imperfection
of any mode of life wherein the end itself is earthly joy is,
after all, an *exemplum* of *cupiditas* by medieval definition),
but the two critics are asking us to read the poem in
widely different ways. In Muscatine's view the irony does
not entirely prevent the poet's ostensible viewpoint from
being his real viewpoint: the attitudes he depicts with
apparent approval still remain 'admirable' though they
are 'incomplete', and, *sub specie aeternitatis*, imperfect.
In Robertson's view the ostensible viewpoint is not the
real viewpoint: the whole intention of the narrative is
ironical and moralistic—to illustrate the idolatrous nature
of the love, and thus to point the distinction between
cupiditas and *caritas*. It is in this way that he finds the poem
to be an allegory. 'Allegory' is a term used so freely now in
criticism—of almost any work of literature that has a
'meaning'—that it need not in itself be the point at issue,
but as Robertson uses the term it entails reading the poem
in a radically new way, as saying one thing to mean
another. This is a 'variant interpretation' that conflicts so
strongly with earlier interpretations that it cries out for
investigation.

R. E. Kaske concluded his review of Robertson's
Preface to Chaucer by asking two questions:

First, what kinds of relationship are possible between the
literal and the extra-literal meanings in literary allegory, and

[1] 'Chaucerian Tragedy', *ELH* xix (1952), pp. 11–37; and *A Preface to
Chaucer* (Princeton Univ. Press, Oxford Univ. Press, 1963), pp. 472–502,
et passim.

how direct can we normally expect this relationship to be . . . ? And secondly, to what extent does this 'allegory' produce a continuous level of meaning beyond the literal, and to what extent merely a number of separate allusions.[1]

These are important questions as they might be applied to individual poems, but I doubt the usefulness of the exercise they propose, in so far as it might be expected to produce evidence for what we may 'normally expect' of medieval literary allegory. For if we are to revive for the term 'allegory', as Robertson does, all the earlier senses covered by the term *allegoria*, the scope of possible forms is so wide that no definition could be found to fit them all that would not be so indefinite as to tell us practically nothing. *Allegoria*, in fact, need not involve extra-literal meaning, strictly speaking, at all: it can take the form of enigmatic expression in which what seems to be said is not really what is actually said, or of ironic ambiguity in which what is actually said is more than what seems to be said. In either form it is not the literal, but the prima-facie meaning that is not the real meaning, or not the only meaning. For example, if the description of the earlier stages of Troilus' love for Criseyde is, as Robertson's allegorical interpretation holds, an ironical depiction of the processes of *cupiditas*, or abuse of beauty, as defined by St. Augustine ('suggestion' or 'sight', followed by contemplation with a view to fleshly satisfaction, leading to 'consent' if reason relinquishes its natural function),[2] it is 'allegorical', not because we must seek an extra-literal meaning in the depiction itself, but because what seems on the face of it a depiction of the processes of 'romantic' or 'courtly' love

---

[1] 'Chaucer and Medieval Allegory', *ELH* xxx (1963), p. 192.

[2] See Robertson, *Preface to Chaucer*, pp. 72 ff.; and for the application to Troilus, pp. 476 ff.

follows so closely the Augustinian pattern of *cupiditas* as to suggest that this was the signification designed by the poet. The signification is not a figurative one: the processes depicted are, on a quite literal level, identifiable with the processes of cupidity—if we choose to look at them in that way. The picture is like those black and white trick pictures that present different things according to whether the black part is seen as the object and the white as the background, or vice versa: both 'objects', the pattern of love familiar in courtly romances and the pattern of cupidity, can be seen in the same picture, and that is why it is possible to speak of its ambiguity in Empson's definition—'We call it ambiguous, I think, when we recognize that there could be a puzzle as to what the author meant, in that alternative views might be taken without sheer misreading.'[1] But such a definition of course begs the question of what we mean by 'misreading'. The alternative views of the 'meaning' of *Troilus and Criseyde* have been taken without misreading, if we mean by that failure to understand Chaucer's English, but failure to understand what that English is intended to convey is misreading of another kind.

Robertson attributes what he regards as failure on the part of critics to perceive the intrinsic irony of Chaucer's narrative partly to their failure to share the medieval assumptions of the poet (through mistaken assumptions about the 'romantic' or 'idealistic' nature of so-called 'courtly love' poetry), and partly to failure to understand and recognize the medieval tropes of *allegoria*. And he sees the second failure as an inevitable consequence of the first:

The difficulty lies in the fact that allegory in this sense must

---

[1] Preface to the 2nd edn. of *Seven Types of Ambiguity*, p. x.

rest on an assumed sense of values. When the values upon which such tropes are based are not understood, or when more modern values are assumed for the text, the tropes themselves disappear, and we are left with 'literal' statements.[1]

There is certainly some truth in this, but I think it is an overstatement. If it were entirely true it would mean that the clues to the tropes are wholly external—that a modern reader must take the underlying ironic meaning as it were on trust, solely on the grounds that it would have been clear to a medieval audience. And fortunately this is not so. Many, if not all, the medieval tropes of *allegoria* are recognizable modes of ironic expression today, though we do not isolate them and give them names as carefully as did the medieval grammarians.[2] But more important, I think, is that in Chaucer's ironies there are usually specific hints of some sort, in the trope itself or in the context, to provide the clues to the values or assumptions implied. To take an easy example—when Chaucer writes of the Monk in the Prologue to the *Canterbury Tales*, 'And I seyde his opinion was good', he is probably using *anti-phrasis*, as Robertson suggests, but we do not need a previous knowledge of medieval assumptions about monks to detect the irony: it is clear enough from the speciousness of the arguments used to support the *antiphrasis*, which Robertson himself indeed points out.[3] And it is a specious-ness that does not rest entirely on medieval assumptions:

---

[1] *Preface to Chaucer*, p. 288.

[2] Payne writes similarly of Chaucer's style in a larger sense, in his discussion of the structure of *Troilus*: 'If, for a while, we talk about selection, amplification, and abbreviation as ways of reconstructing an old story so that a fitting style can distribute through it the particular decorative emphasis which will reactivate it, we are not necessarily talking about things visible only through a singularly astigmatic medieval eye' (*The Key of Remembrance*, p. 176).

[3] *Preface to Chaucer*, p. 255.

the question, 'How shal the world be served ?' (if a monk
stays in his cloister) certainly takes on a deeper irony when
we know that it was a question debated in the Middle
Ages in the more important issue of whether monks
should take secular offices, but the immediate irony lies
in applying it to this monk whose activities outside the
cloister may seem to be legitimate enough, but are described
in such ambiguous terms as to suggest other activities to
which the question would hardly be relevant. The irony
may depend in part on extra-literal meaning, if, for
example, as Robertson suggests, there is an iconographic
significance in the 'deyntee hors' he had in stable, and the
'hare' he hunted, but for the most part it is by careful attention to what the text actually says (for example, the ambiguity of 'venerie' and 'prikyng') that the modern reader
can detect the irony.

Irony presents much more of a problem, however, when
it is sustained irony, pervading an entire work, or the greater
part of it. For if the irony is maintained consistently it will
present a consistent front which may easily be taken at its
face value, since the clues to the irony must be unobtrusive
if the front is to be maintained convincingly. H. W.
Fowler defined irony as 'a form of utterance that postulates
a double audience, consisting of one party that hearing
shall hear and shall not understand, and another party
that, when more is meant than meets the ear, is aware
both of that more and of the outsiders' incomprehension'.[1]
But in an ironic narrative much must depend on who the
outsider is. When Pandarus offers to help Troilus to win
whatever lady it may be who is causing his suffering,
Troilus replies:

[1] *A Dictionary of Modern English Usage*[2] (Oxford Univ. Press, 1965), s.v.
Irony.

> Ye, so seystow, . . . allas,   (1. 834)
> But god woot, it is naught the rather so;
> Ful hard were it to helpen in this cas . . .[1]

Here it is Pandarus who is the outsider, and Troilus and the reader who are the other party; but in the event Pandarus by no means finds it hard to help, and on this level it is Troilus who is the outsider. In dramatic irony of this kind the reader is always in the secret, but when the whole method of narration is ironic, so that the author himself must speak with a double voice (that of the outsider and that of the other party), where does the reader stand ? If the irony is obvious there is no problem—as Empson puts it, 'even the most obvious irony is a sort of playing at deception, but it may imply that only a comic butt could be deceived'.[2] If the expression is more enigmatic, but nevertheless of such a kind that it is possible to detect with reasonable certainty that what is said in apparent good faith either does not mean what it seems to mean, or is demonstrably false, the problem becomes one of careful reading. But there is a still less obvious kind of ironic narration where the double form of utterance makes for what is a real, and not only a stylistic, ambiguity. For an ironic narrator is presenting, at one and the same time, more than one way of looking at the same thing, and he may choose to leave us in some doubt as to which viewpoint he is asking us to take (as in some of the novels of Henry James). Irony of this kind can be a way of throwing the onus of moral judgement on to the reader, or of bringing home to him more actively the complexity of the issues involved. But it is a hazard of this least obvious kind of ironic narration (and not only of medieval 'allegory') that stories

---

[1] Text from R. K. Root's edn. (Princeton, 1926).
[2] Preface to the 2nd edn. of *Seven Types of Ambiguity*, p. x.

presented in this way become peculiarly liable to variant interpretation according to the assumptions the reader brings to bear on them about the values, premisses, and modes of expression he finds in them. When Pandarus is trying to convince Troilus that it will not be too difficult to win Criseyde, he argues:

> . . . sith thy lady vertuous is al,   (1. 898)
> So foloweth it that there is som pitee
> Amonges alle thise other in general;
> And forthi se that thow in special
> Requere nat that is ayeyns hyre name,
> For vertu streccheth nat hym self to shame.

Those who see the story as a story of idealistic, noble courtly love will find nothing odd in Criseyde's virtue being brought forward as an argument here, and hence nothing wrong with the argument itself; for if Criseyde 'vertuous is al' her virtues must include pity (the 'coroune of vertues alle'), and it is reasonable to argue that if virtue brings shame on itself it is no longer a virtue.[1] But those who see irony in the idea of a virtuousness that may include the kind of 'pitee' Pandarus has in mind will find specious or perverse the argument that such a virtue stretches itself to shame only if there is public scandal.[2] Thus those who assume (or do not assume) irony in Chaucer's viewpoint to his story will find (or not find) it in his mode of expres-sion in this passage. And this circularity operates at all levels of the narrative. For it is from variant interpretation of such passages in turn that variant interpretations of 'character' are, if not born, at least nurtured. C. S. Lewis,

[1] See Root, note to 1. 897–903.
[2] Robertson writes of this passage: 'Virtue may "stretch itself" to the kind of "pity" May shows for Damyan, and in Pandarus' view it will not reach the point of "shame" unless someone else finds out about it'. (*Preface*, p. 480.)

who regards the loves in the story as 'so nobly conceived that they are divided only by the thinnest partition from the lawful loves of Dorigen and her husband', sees Pandarus as 'a friend according to the old, high code of friendship, and a man of sentiment. The "ironic" Pandarus is not to be found in the pages of Chaucer'.[1] Whereas Robertson writes:

The character of Pandarus is a masterpiece of medieval irony. On the surface, he is an attractive little man, wise, witty, and generous. But his wisdom is not of the kind that Lady Philosophy would approve, and his generosity is of the type which supplies gold to the avaricious and dainties to the glutton. . . . Indeed, there is more than a suggestion in the poem that Pandarus is a blind leader of the blind, a priest of Satan.[2]

There would be less scope for such divergent views if what Chaucer has to say in his person as narrator were not itself ambiguous. To take one of the less complex examples —when Troilus and Criseyde are in bed together for the first time, the narrator interrupts his story to profess his incompetence to describe their joy—'juggeth, ye that han ben at the feste'—and proceeds with an invocation:

> O blisful nyght, of hem so longe isought,   (III. 1317)
> How blithe unto hem bothe two thow weere!
> Why ne hadde I swich oon with my soule ybought,
> Ye, or the leeste joie that was there?

This could be just the hyperbolic expression of envy of the lovers' joy that it seems to be, or it could be ironic, with its oblique reminder of how such joy may have to be paid for. If it is ironic, the poet is speaking with a double voice,

[1] *The Allegory of Love* (Clarendon Press, 1936), pp. 197 and 191.
[2] *Preface*, p. 479.

that of the narrator unaware of the implication of his words, and that of the author aware both of the implication and of the narrator's unawareness. This of course is only another way of saying what has already been said in some recent criticism, that Chaucer's narrator is a man of straw. E. Talbot Donaldson, for example, has shown how 'Chaucer has manipulated a narrator capable of only a simple view of reality in such a way as to achieve the poetic expression of an extraordinarily complex one'.[1] This is one way of looking at it, and when we see the poem in these terms it is certainly necessary to distinguish between narrator and poet. But they are terms too wide to be of much practical help in the interpretation of specific complexities in the poetry itself, and it is when we come to try to analyse specific passages that we see that the manipulation of the narrator is really a process of giving to what he says, both in his own interventions and in his narrative, the verbal ambiguities by which the poet expresses his own complex viewpoint. And in this aspect we cannot separate narrator from poet. For example, in the passage just quoted the narrator's attitude is one of evident admiration of the lovers' joy—indeed the passage has sometimes been cited as evidence that 'Chaucer himself' approves of the love in the story—and to perceive the irony of giving the narrator this simple view must be to see him as a *persona* distinct from the poet; but unless we perceive also the verbal ambiguity of his comment, we miss what specific clues there may be to the meaning of the irony, to its intent. It is an ambiguity that gives room for alternative reactions, in that the narrator's address to that 'blisful nyght' can be

---

[1] 'The ending of Chaucer's *Troilus*', *Early English and Norse Studies, Presented to Hugh Smith in Honour of his Sixtieth Birthday*, ed. Arthur Brown and Peter Foote (Methuen, 1963), p. 43.

read just as the hyperbolic expression of envy that it seems to be, or the last two lines of it can be seen as the time-honoured trick of using a rhetorical question ironically to give the hint to its own answer. The meaning of the passage probably lies in the ambiguity itself. For, by using a narrator capable of only a simple view of the situation in such a way as to express a more complex one, the poet is putting two views to the reader, leaving him to take the one his perception, intellectual and moral, leads him to take. Robert Payne has observed that 'the kinds of roles Chaucer creates for his narrators almost necessarily imply complementary roles for an audience which is nearly as much a created fiction within or around the poem as the narrator is'. His view is that the narrator's interventions to address the audience are a way of making any reader 'feel specifically included in the audience, without exactly realizing that the feeling of inclusion is also an admission of qualities in himself which place him within the range of the poem's judgements'.[1] This applies to what Payne calls the narrator's 'self-deprecatory ironies', which assume in the members of the audience a greater experience of love than his own, and appeal to them to supply for themselves what he professes himself incapable of supplying. But, as the example just quoted may illustrate, the ambiguities of the narrator's interventions may leave it open to the reader to identify with the lovers or to perceive the warning, implicit in the ambiguity, not to identify. On the one hand there is the self-deprecatory appeal to the audience—'jug-geth, ye that han ben at the feste'—and on the other hand there are all the ingredients for irony—the rhetorical fervency of the narrator's invocation to that 'blisful nyght', and the ironic betrayal, the hint that something is being

[1] *The Key of Remembrance*, p. 228.

expressed at the expense of his attitude. Yet the effect is more comic than satiric, and not enough to destroy the emotional impression—largely because it is only a hint. There is no clear pointer to a moralistic view; only a verbal ambiguity that gives the reader the amusement of detecting a possible hidden meaning, while leaving it to him to decide if, or how seriously, it is intended.

The function of the ambiguity in the narrative is even more relevant where the larger issues of the poem's meaning are involved. For illicit sexual joy is child's play compared with these: the 'moralitee' is concerned less with the fact that it is love outside marriage than with the nature of the love itself. If we see no ambiguity in the depiction, if we take at its face value the attitude of approval that the description of the love seems to suggest, there is a disparity, an incongruity between the narrative and the 'moralitee' of the epilogue, which some have seen as an artistic failure on the part of the poet;[1] some have explained by assuming the epilogue to be a palinode (a retraction of the ideals of 'courtly love' in the narrative); and some by finding in the poem a 'triple scale of values', by which the courtly love it depicts is distinguished, on the one hand, by its *gentilesse*, from lust, and on the other hand, *sub specie aeternitatis*, from the Christian ideal of love or *caritas*. In Robertson's allegorical interpretation of the narrative as an ironical depiction of *cupiditas*, the epilogue becomes the logical conclusion of the poem, defining explicitly the distinction between *cupiditas* and *caritas* that the narrative was designed to illustrate. In one aspect, this interpretation is only facing

---

[1] This view, which might be thought to have been killed by more recent criticism, has been revived by Margaret Schlauch: '. . . one might argue that the final palinode required a better preparation reaching back to the earlier parts of the poem', *Antecedents of the English Novel: 1400–1600* (Oxford Univ. Press, 1963), p. 39, n.

the fact that, if we are to credit Chaucer with knowing what he was doing when he wrote his epilogue, we are bound to accept that, in terms of the Christian doctrine of love it defines, the kind of love his story depicts must be *cupiditas*, and therefore it is reasonable to approach the poem with at least a suspicion that there is irony in his depiction of the love with apparent approval. But the suspicion should not be an assumption: it is only by testing the suspicion, from within the narrative itself, that we can hope to detect the function of the irony in the total effect of the poem—and it may prove to be a less simple function than we might expect.

But how exactly—by what criteria—can a reader test his suspicion that Chaucer's depiction of his love story with apparent approval is ironic, that the poem may be a moral allegory? In a contribution to the controversy on allegory in medieval and renaissance literature (no doubt stimu‑ lated to some extent by Robertson's thesis), Rhodes Dunlap cites passages from Bacon's Preface to his essays *Of the Wisdom of the Ancients* which suggest 'two positive criteria' for use by the allegorical interpreter. The first is what Dunlap calls 'congruity': Bacon writes that what has con‑ vinced him that 'a concealed instruction and allegory was originally intended in many of the ancient fables' is that :

In the very frame and texture of the story as in the propriety of the names by which the persons that figure in it are distin‑ guished, I find a conformity and connexion with the thing signified, so close and so evident, that one cannot help believ‑ ing such a signification to have been designed and meditated from the first, and purposely shadowed out.

The second criterion, on the contrary, is what Dunlap calls 'a kind of incongruity within the suspectedly alle‑ gorical narrative'. Bacon writes :

There is yet another sign, and one of no small value, that these fables contain a hidden and involved meaning; which is, that some of them are so absurd and stupid on the face of the narrative taken by itself, that they may be said to give notice from afar and cry out that there is a parable below.[1]

There is also a third criterion suggested by Bacon in this Preface when he adds:

> But the argument of most weight with me is this, that many of these fables by no means appear to have been invented by the persons who relate and divulge them. . . . Besides, as they are differently related by writers nearly of the same ages, it is easily perceived that the relators drew from the common stock of ancient tradition, and varied but in point of embellishment, which is their own.

It is of course a far cry from the kind of allegorical fable Bacon had in mind to *Troilus and Criseyde*, and yet I think the three criteria he suggests can usefully be applied to that poem. The first—that of 'congruity'—is indeed the one applied by Robertson, notably when he finds in the depic- tion of Troilus' love a conformity with the pattern of *cupiditas* in the medieval definition. But when he insists that such depictions can have only a moralistic significance, and are not to be read in terms of their 'psychological' insight, or as 'characterization', he lays his thesis open to criticism. For leaving aside the question of how it is possible to convey moralistic significance in terms of human behaviour and attitudes or thoughts without also conveying psychological processes and 'character', we may feel that such a limited view fails to do justice to Chaucer's narrative art (and indeed to his moralistic intention). If the story is an allegory we have certainly come a long way

[1] See 'The Allegorical Interpretation of Renaissance Literature', *PMLA* lxxxii (1967), p. 41.

from the kind of allegory that depends on such arbitrary factors as 'the propriety of the names by which the persons are distinguished'. If there is an allegorical meaning it is made to emerge from the reactions of the persons themselves to each important turn of events, and this must give a new intrinsic importance to 'character', even when it is con-ceived primarily for its evaluative, or moralistic, function. Chaucer did not of course invent this new form of narrative art: he inherited it from the French romance writers, who had developed not only this method of revealing subtleties of character and motive in their stories, but also what Eugène Vinaver calls 'the habit of expressing through a *fabula* or a *historia* a point of view of their own'. They use their stories 'to serve as an expression of the thoughts and emotions inspired by courtly idealism, to translate in terms of actions and characters the subtle varieties of courtly sentiment and the highly sophisticated code of courtly behaviour'.[1] This may help to explain why Chaucer chose to recast a story so 'unlykely' for courtly romance (a story of fickle love) in such highly courtly terms. For while the action lends itself well to his Christian 'moralitee', at the same time he can demonstrate that morality more interestingly and more amusingly by applying it to the idealism of the world of courtly lovers. His view of his story therefore comes to include social attitudes and philosophies that belong to that world—at least in literature. For unless it can be proved that all 'courtly love' literature has an ironic, moralistic intent, the kind of courtly idealism his story depicts must be assumed to have a real (non-allegorical) existence. It is a weakness of Robertson's presentation of his case that he assumes (unnecessarily) that so-called 'courtly love' literature in

[1] *The Works of Sir Thomas Malory* (Clarendon Press, 1947), vol. 1, pp. lxiv–v.

general has an allegorical, moralistic intent, since this is something that he does not, and indeed could not, prove. It is not proof to demonstrate a congruity between the pattern of courtly love and the pattern of *cupiditas*, unless it can be shown that it was the intention of the author to reveal that congruity. And this is what must be demonstrated in *Troilus*—from within the poem itself—if the allegorical interpretation is to be convincing. If the narration is ironical, it is irony that takes us into the mental world of the persons in the story, pretending to accept their values, their premisses, their methods of reasoning. To demonstrate that the picture is ironical we must show, not only that it is really a picture of *cupiditas*, but that the values, the premisses, and the modes of expression themselves reveal this. And this is where the second criterion, that of 'incongruity within the suspectedly allegorical narrative', comes in. For if we take as the criterion of 'congruity' a conformity or connection with the Christian distinction between *caritas* and *cupiditas* expressed or implied in the epilogue, we must look, not for a direct conformity, but for incongruities, absurd or puzzling features, which nevertheless add up to a congruity in that what they betray is the opposition between the courtly concept of love that is ostensibly being depicted and the Christian concept that is being, ironically, revealed. And to this end we must look particularly at those 'points of embellishment' which are Chaucer's own (Bacon's third criterion): when he tampers with his sources, whether it is his main source for the narrative, Boccaccio's *Il Filostrato*, or those sources on which he draws for many of his own embellishments (Boethius, or the *Roman de la Rose*, or Dante, for example), we must look not only at the more obvious changes he may make, but at what may appear to be pointless alterations—

transpositions and the like. Chaucer is too good a poet to do anything without an ulterior motive, and such apparently trivial alterations can be valuable pointers to his intention.

His ironic method in this poem, as elsewhere in his poetry, can often be analysed in terms of the tropes described by the medieval grammarians, and an acquaintance with these tropes may be useful, though I do not think it is essential, in detecting his irony. For example, to recognize the various rhetorical devices for avoiding naming a thing by its proper name, or hiding a disagreeable sense under an agreeable expression, can help the reader to see more clearly through the veil of courtly language, especially in the early books. Similarly if we know that *prosecutio cum proverbiis* was recognized by medieval rhetoricians as one of the ways of presenting an argument misleadingly, we are more likely to treat with caution the many passages in the poem where an argument is given plausibility by proverbs (and Pandarus is not the only one to use proverbs freely). We must be alive also to the possibility of other kinds of specious dialectic—where for example, one argument does not really follow from another, or where the evidence cited does not prove what it purports to prove, or where the argument used does not really apply to the case in hand. It will be shown in the following chapters that all these are among the ironic methods Chaucer uses in the narrative. But, most important of all, we must be aware of the possible ambiguity of his use of the word 'love'. Some time ago D. W. Robertson remarked: 'The fact that the word love (*amor*) could be used for either Charity or cupidity opened enormous possibilities for literary word-play.'[1]

---

[1] 'The Doctrine of Charity in Medieval Literary Gardens', *Speculum*, xxvi (1951), p. 28.

But it would be wrong to describe the semantic deception of Chaucer's use of the word in this poem in such simple terms. 'Love' can be used both of the natural impulse that makes us love and of the emotional feeling we have when we desire something or someone. It is not without cause that critics of the stature of C. S. Lewis have felt the poem to be the great hymn of praise to love that it seems to be, but more recent analysis of it in the light of medieval philosophy has made it easier to see that what seems to be an exaltation of the love passion the lovers feel may really be an exaltation of the impulse of love itself. P. M. Kean writes of the poem:

. . . its subject is, surely, a love which is only part of the divinely implanted tendency of the human soul to strive to return to its true source, a tendency which finds partial satis⁄ faction in earthly love, and which, since it is part of something inherently good, must result in ultimate good for the soul which 'ne hath nat al foryeten itself', and which preserves some knowledge of its true descent.[1]

But while this may be true of the medieval philosophy of love which informs the poem, it is also true, in terms of that philosophy, that the 'partial satisfaction' found in earthly love can only be an illusory happiness (and not a finding of true 'good'), if the love has lost its true direction. All love is an 'entencioun to comen to good', but what is at issue in *Troilus and Criseyde* is whether the 'entencioun' of the lovers was blind, whether the good they were seeking was the true good. If it was not, then their love must be *cupiditas*, in terms of the medieval doctrine. But it is not simply the fact that the word 'love' could be used for either *caritas* or *cupiditas* that makes the ambiguity of its use possible: it is also the paradox inherent in the medieval

[1] 'Chaucer's Dealings with a Stanza of *Il Filostrato* and the Epilogue of *Troilus and Criseyde*', *Medium Aevum*, xxxiii (1964), p. 46.

philosophy of love itself, by which all love, being a divinely implanted impulse of the soul, is good of its own nature, even though it may be perverted from its true end (the 'good' it is seeking) into a love of a false good.

Chaucer's revelation of his meaning depends in large measure on the way in which he uses Boethius' *Consola-tion of Philosophy*, the influence of which is evident every-where in the poem—in the surface texture (echoes of phraseology and figures of speech), in longer passages which are more or less close paraphrases, as well as in the choice of general topics or motifs which constitute an over-all pattern of relevance to the story. But almost all this Boethian material is used ironically, in that what it seems to be saying is different from what it says if we refer it to its proper context in the *Consolation*. In this way it serves as a 'congruity' to show up the 'incongruities' of the values, premisses, and attitudes of the persons in the story into whose mouths it is put. Robertson observes, with truth, that 'it is impossible to idealize passionate love for a gift of Fortune in Boethian terms', but the method by which Chaucer appears to be doing just this is the am-biguous method by which his meaning becomes richer and fuller. This is what I hope to demonstrate in the next chapter, and my excuse for going over ground that has already been tilled. But I would not wish it to be thought that I am claiming what Bacon claims in his Preface already referred to:

The like indeed has been attempted by others; but to speak ingenuously, their great and voluminous labours have almost destroyed the energy, the efficacy, and grace of the thing . . . they have applied the sense of the parables to certain general and vulgar matters, without reaching to their real import, genuine interpretation, and full depth.

What I have to offer is no new 'genuine interpretation', only an attempt to clarify a little more, and perhaps con-firm or modify, as the case may be, interpretations that have been offered before, by examining in greater detail than has yet been done Chaucer's methods of using his Boethian material in this poem.

CHAPTER II

Ambiguity and Boethius

WHEN 'Boethius' puts his complaint to Philosophia in the *Consolation of Philosophy*, he is suffering unjustly (as he feels) from a severe reversal of his fortunes, and she answers him with arguments to prove that what he has lost—fame, honours, riches—are only 'false goods'. And having demonstrated this at some length, she adds:

> But what schal I seye of delyces of body, of whiche delices the desirynges ben ful of anguyssch, and the fulfillynges of hem ben ful of penance? How grete seknesses and how grete sorwes unsuffrable, ryght as a maner fruyt of wykkidnesse, ben thilke delices wont to bryngen to the bodyes of folk that usen hem! Of whiche delices I not what joie mai ben had of here moevynge, but this woot I wel, that whosoevere wol remembren hym of his luxures, he schal wel undirstonden that the issues of delices ben sorweful and sorye. And yif thilke delices mowen maken folk blisful, thanne by the same cause moten thise beestis ben clepid blisful, of whiche beestes al the entencioun hasteth to fulfille here bodily jolyte.[1]

It may well have been because 'delices of body' was not as relevant as fame, honours, riches to the situation of 'Boethius' that she puts it last in her list of 'false goods', and treats it much more briefly. But when she goes on immediately to say that 'the gladnesse of wyf and children were an honest thyng, but it hath ben seyd that it is over-

---

[1] III, prosa 7, in Chaucer's translation, F. N. Robinson, *The Works of Geoffrey Chaucer*, 2nd edn. (Boston, Houghton Mifflin, 1957), pp. 346-7.

mochel ayens kynde that children han ben fownden tor-
mentours to here fadris . . .', we may feel that the author's
interest in 'delices of body' as it concerns sexual desire is a
narrow, almost perfunctory one.

By the time that Chaucer wrote his *Troilus* there had
been a change in philosophical attitude or emphasis,
brought about no doubt by many various factors, but
among them certainly a greater preoccupation of philosophical thought with the problem of love, and a clearer
understanding of the human aspect. The newer medieval
philosophies of love of the twelfth and thirteenth centuries
owe much to the *Consolation*, and they reach what are
essentially the same philosophical conclusions, but they
reach them by a different route, and define the relation
between human and divine love in terms which make the
concept more comprehensible on the practical level. It is a
relation which lies at the very core of Christianity, but at
no time has that fact been realized as clearly, and defined
as unmistakably, as it was in the Middle Ages. The preoccupation of medieval literature with the subject of love
derives, above all, from the preoccupation of philosophers
and theologians who brought it to the fore, and thus
opened up the subject for exploration in the world of
poetry and art, where the Christian philosophy of love can
be applied to a wide range of human activity. Poets like
Alain de Lille and Jean de Meun can make their own
poetic explorations in a new climate of thought where love
of any kind, even illicit sexual love, is regarded as worthy
of being treated at length as an aspect of human activity
and a problem of human behaviour posing philosophical
questions that did not come into the purview of Boethius,
or at least not in that form. It was from such poetry, as well
as from Boethius, that Chaucer learnt the theory of love,

and it was in this new climate of thought that he was attracted into making his own poetic explorations. When he interprets the Troilus story in the light of the Boethian distinction between true and false happiness, he is not only using the *Consolation* directly but also as it had been used before, especially in the *Roman de la Rose*, and it is in the light of the newer philosophies of love that he applies the Boethian ideas.

Where he surpasses the earlier poets is in the more subtle and more comprehensive use he makes of the *Consolation* to give, ironically, a philosophical coherence to his theme. And the plan and structure of the *Consolation* lend them-selves in several ways to his ironic use of it. Although Boethius propounds philosophical ideas so closely con-forming to Christian doctrine that for centuries his book was one of the most authoritative among theologians, he aims to reach his conclusions by reasoning—drawn mainly from pre-Christian thought, Platonic, Aristotelian, and Neoplatonic—without recourse to revelation or theological terminology. And Chaucer was not the first poet to exploit this 'non-Christian' language of the *Consolation* for ironic purposes, using arguments, images, figures of speech in a way that perverts their real meaning. In *Troilus* there are many ironic echoes of this kind on the textual surface; but Chaucer goes much further than this. He exploits, ironic-ally, the relevance to his story of the three main topics of the *Consolation*—the relation of Fortune to Providence, of true to false happiness, and the problem of reconciling God's foreknowledge with man's free will; and he does so by exploiting the method by which Philosophia uses these topics to give to 'Boethius' his 'consolation' (a fuller understanding of the nature and working of Providence). For she begins with what she calls her 'lyghtere medicynes', easy arguments comprehensible from the world of human affairs, before she goes on to her 'strengere medicynes', the more abstruse and spiritual material; and, as was usual in medieval disputation, her 'pupil' at each stage puts his problem first as he sees it, and his 'mistress' then explains where he has gone wrong. This general plan makes it possible to abstract passages that are misleading out of their context; and this is what Chaucer does consistently in his narrative: he uses arguments from the *Consolation*, usually in close paraphrase, on all three topics dealt with there, as though unaware of what the full implications of those arguments must be in terms of Philosophia's conclusions, when applied to the situations to which he applies them in his story. It is an extended use of the method he was to use later in the Wife of Bath's prologue, when she quotes theological authorities in a way that perverts their real meaning.

As an example of how the method has contributed to the ironic ambiguity of the poem, we may take the second topic of the *Consolation*—the relation between true and false happiness—which is explained in Book III, after the defence of Fortune in II. All men know that happiness is the supreme good, and all men seek it by natural impulse. This is the 'natural enclyning' of the soul, which comes from heaven, to return to its home: it is compared with the struggle of a caged bird to return to the woods (metrum 2). But it is with 'dyrkyd memorie' that men seek, like a drunk man who does not know the way home; and 'mys-wandrynge errour' leads them into seeking the happiness that is the supreme good in what are only 'false goods', since they are only partial and undependable sources of happiness—such as riches, honours, fame, or 'delices of body'. Yet the very fact that they seek happiness in this way shows 'how greet is the strengthe of nature', for what they are really seeking is the whole and perfect happiness ('algates men accorden alle in lovynge the eende of good', prosa 2). But although these false goods may give some inkling of the supreme good, in which perfect happiness lies, they are not parts of it in the way that members of the body are parts of the whole body: Philosophia shows by stages of reasoning (including the axiom that all perfect things must be prior to all imperfect things) that the supreme and perfect good is in God, and is therefore indivisible. The happiness that the false goods bring, therefore, can only be a deceptive and mutable happiness: true and permanent happiness can only come by participa⁄ tion in the whole and perfect good that is in God.

It is the philosophies of the twelfth and thirteenth centuries that make clearer what this means in relation to human love. God is both what we love and what makes us love it, since the cause of our love is the love of himself he implanted in our being when he created us. It follows then that to love any good is always to love its resemblance to the Divine and Perfect Goodness, since it is this resemblance that makes it into a good. The problem of human love therefore is to recognize itself for what it is, know its objective, and keep itself from being deflected from it. For if man knows, as he is capable of knowing by his reason, that what he loves on the human level is really the resemblance of God, he cannot love the resemblance without loving even more what it resembles. It is in this way that man can love on the human level 'for the sake of God', or that love of a creature can lead towards love of the Creator—but only if what is loved is the divine resemblance, the goodness that is in God. Since true happiness can be found only in the progression of the soul towards the Love

whence it came, love of a creature, if it is love for the sake
of something other than the divine resemblance, can only
prevent that progression, and therefore cannot lead to true
happiness.

Chaucer draws attention to this Christian philosophy of
love by various oblique allusions throughout his story.
For example, his narrator remarks, on that 'blisful nyght':

> Felicite, which that thise clerkes wise   (III. 1691)
> Comenden so, ne may nat here suffise.

Ostensibly he is exalting the lovers' happiness, but when
we know that the happiness the wise clerks commend is
the perfect happiness the irony is clear. Similarly Chaucer
gives to Criseyde the arguments used by Philosophia to
show that worldly happiness cannot be true happiness.
The immediate occasion for Criseyde's speech is a part of
the strategy by which Pandarus is contriving to get
Troilus into the bedroom where Criseyde has retired for
the night. He comes to tell her that Troilus (who has been
hidden in an inner closet) has just arrived in great distress
because he has heard that Criseyde loves 'oon that hatte
Horaste'. Criseyde's speech on 'worldly selynesse | Which
clerkes callen fals felicitee' refers to the 'wikked serpent,
jalousie' which apparently has come to spoil their happiness: she is dismayed that her 'deere herte' should believe
the story, and reflects that worldly happiness 'Imedled is
with many a bitternesse', since it is either not complete or
not lasting. If we know it is not lasting we can never be
free from fear of losing it. If we do not know, how can we
call it true happiness when it rests on ignorance! If we do
not care a mite if we should lose it the happiness cannot be
worth much. Therefore, she concludes: 'trewely, for
aught I kan espie, | Ther is no verray weele in this world

heere' (III. 813-36). The arguments by which Criseyde reaches this conclusion are those used by Philosophia in her 'lyghtere medicynes' to show how, even on the worldly level only, it must be clear that worldly happiness is not true happiness; but Philosophia does not conclude therefore, as Criseyde does, that there is no true happiness in this world: in her 'strengere medicynes' she explains what true happiness in this world is. Criseyde's speech is consistent with her character as we have seen it, for example, in her long soliloquy on the pros and cons of entering into a love relation with Troilus (II. 701-812), and in her remarks on the falsity of this world (II. 410 and 420). In her mouth the Boethian arguments contribute to the impression of her cautious attitude to life, her excessive fear of being let down.[1] But it is typical of the close connection there is in the poem between 'character' and moralistic meaning that Criseyde's speech here reveals that her understanding does not go beyond the worldly view. And the irony that gives this proof of the falsity of worldly happiness to the one who was to be the instrument of the proof in action, later in the story, adds stylistic point to its relevance to the present situation.

A still more important use of the topics of the *Consolation* comes in the references in the third book to love as a universal principle—the 'holy bond of love'. There are three such major references in that book: in the hymn to love in the Proem (1-49); in Troilus' address of thanksgiving to love (1254-74); and in his hymn to love (1744-71). The concept itself derives directly from the *Consola*

---

[1] It is easy, however, to read too much 'psychology' into such passages: B. L. Jefferson writes: 'Finally, Criseyde, who is thus so keenly conscious of the falsity of worldly hopes, by a kind of autosuggestion becomes false herself', *Chaucer and the Consolation of Philosophy of Boethius* (Princeton, 1917), p. 129.

tion, notably from Book II, metrum 8; and Chaucer had
found it already in *Il Filostrato* in the song that Troilo sings
in celebration of love (3. 74–9). It was this song that
Chaucer used for his Proem, and he inserted in its place
Troilus' hymn (1744–71), which is a close paraphrase of
the Boethian metrum almost in its entirety. This hymn
does not appear in all the manuscripts of *Troilus*, and was
almost certainly inserted by Chaucer in a revision of his
poem.[1] Why did Chaucer make this revision? Why, for
that matter, did he move Troilo's song to the Proem in the
first place? Like Troilo's song, the Proem is an invocation
to Venus praising her beneficent powers, and in it there is
an apparent confusion, or blending, of the pagan goddess
('Joves doughter deere') with the planet Venus, evidently
thought of as the agent of divine, or cosmic, love:

> In hevene and helle, in erthe and salte see,   (III. 8)
> Is felt thi myght, if that I wel descerne;
> As man, brid, best, fisshe, herbe, and grene tree
> The fele in tymes with vapour eterne.
> God loveth, and to love wol nat werne;
> And in this world no lyves creature,
> Withouten love, is worth, or may endure.

And in the next stanza Venus is even referred to in terms
that seem to suggest the theological concept of the Holy
Spirit vivifying and impersonating the Love of God:[2]

> Ye Joves first to thilke effectes glade,   (15)
> Thorugh which that thynges lyven alle and be,
> Comeveden, and amoreux hem made
> On mortal thyng . . .

Whatever may have been Boccaccio's intention in these

[1] See R. K. Root, *The Textual Tradition of Chaucer's Troilus*, Chaucer
Society, xcix, 1st Ser. (London, 1916), pp. 155–7; and *Troilus and Criseyde*,
p. lxxi.   [2] See Root's note to 15–17.

ambiguous passages, Chaucer has certainly increased the
ambiguity by transferring the song to the Proem; for what
in Troilo's mouth has a specific reference to his own
situation, and hence to sexual love specifically, has a more
general, and therefore more ambiguous, reference to love,
as Chaucer places it—as can be seen, for example, when he
substitutes for Troilo's 'Certa cagion del valor che mi
muove' the line 'O verray cause of heele and of gladnesse'
(6). Moreover, Chaucer's Venus is a more ambiguous
figure because he has stripped the poem of much of its
mythological machinery, and imparted at times a kind of
Christian symbolism to what he retains. For example, it is
'heigh Jove' who commits to Fortune 'by purveyance and
disposicioun' the 'permutacioun of thynges' (v. 1541-4).
If Jove himself can be identified in this way with the Christian concept of God, the invocation to 'Joves doughter
deere' becomes ambiguous: the 'love' represented by
Venus becomes less certainly sexual desire only. It is
possible in fact to read the whole invocation either as an
address to the pagan goddess or as an address to Divine
Love. The third stanza, for example, where Venus seems
to be identified with the Holy Spirit, vivifying and impersonating the Love of God, can be read in just that way,
if we think of Jove as Providence. Even those features of
the Proem which may seem to be referring to 'courtly
love' have the same ambiguity. For example, in the
opening stanza, the invocation to 'Joves doughter deere . . .
| In gentil hertes ay redy to repaire' (of which Root
remarks: 'Courtly love was exclusively appropriated to
those of gentle birth') applies also to *caritas*, if we remember
Philosophia's definition of 'gentil' in the third book of the
Consolation.[1] The claims made for the power and bene-

---

[1] See below, p. 56.

ficence of Venus are in fact all of them claims that can be made for the planet Venus, as the agent of Divine Love, as well as (ironically) for the goddess Venus, the personifica- tion of sexual desire. Even the final claim, 'Ye folk a lawe han set in universe . . . | That whoso stryveth with yow hath the werse', is ambiguous, in a way that will be examined more fully in a later chapter.

It may have been the ambiguity inherent in Troilo's song that prompted Chaucer to transfer it to the Proem, for in exploiting its ambiguity he makes of it a fitting introduc- tion to his depiction of love in the third book, which is ostensibly exalting the power and virtue of sexual passion, but in terms that have a similar ironic ambiguity. The ambiguity of Troilo's song may well have been deliberate on its author's part, but Chaucer uses it for a different purpose. And it may be this difference that he is referring to, ironically, when he defends himself in the Prologue to the *Legend of Good Women* against the charge of having offended the god of love by writing his *Troilus*:

> what so myn auctour mente, (G. 460)
> Algate, God wot, it was myn entente
> To forthere trouthe in love, and it cheryce . . .

For, as Robert Payne observes: 'It is precisely what consti- tutes "trouthe in love" that is at issue.'[1]

It was perhaps because Chaucer felt the need to make his meaning clearer that he inserted another hymn for Troilus which, except for a rearrangement of the parts and the alteration of a reference to marriage, reproduces in almost identical terms the Boethian metrum in praise of Divine Love (II. 8).[2] Troilus' hymn is addressed, not to Venus,

[1] *The Key of Remembrance*, p. 109.

[2] See B. L. Jefferson, *Chaucer and the Consolation of Philosophy*, pp. 66–7, for a detailed comparison.

but to 'Love that of erthe and se hath governaunce', which, in the metrum, is God's love which, in creating all things, implanted in them the love that causes them to seek his love. Thus all created activity refers itself necessarily to God's love by virtue of a law implanted in the substance of each being. This law is the 'stable feyth' referred to in the metrum, which Divine Love uses as a controlling force to establish harmony in the universe. As Troilus' hymn puts it, in imagery taken from the metrum, 'if that Love aught lete his bridel go, | Al that now loveth asonder sholde lepe'; for it is by 'feith which that is stable' that 'elementz that ben so discordable | Holden a bond per-petuely durynge', so that the sun has to bring forth 'his rosy day' and the moon have 'lordshipe over the nyghtes', and the sea 'gredy to flowen' has to control its tides (III. 1751-64).

The moralistic relevance of the metrum had come in the last few lines—that it is this same Love that determines the harmony of the human condition, by providing 'lawes' for true friends, and knitting 'sacrement of mariages of chaste loves'. And the concluding sentence, 'O weleful were mankynde, yif thilke love that governeth hevene governede yowr corages', refers to the fact that, unlike the rest of creation, man is free to let his love respond or not respond with 'stable feyth' to the government of Divine Love. When Troilus' hymn transposes the reference to the human condition to the opening stanza, this link becomes less clear. And when it has to substitute for the reference to marriage the vaguer 'Love, that enditeth lawe of com-paignie, | *And couples doth in vertu for to dwelle*', the very fact that the substitution is necessary betrays the inap-plicability to his own love for Criseyde of the 'holy bond of love' his hymn is celebrating, for an illicit relationship cannot, by its very nature, belong to the divine order of harmony.

The concluding stanza of Troilus' hymn does not follow the metrum closely:

> So wolde god, that auctour is of kynde, (1765)
> That, with his bond, Love of his vertu liste
> To cerclen hertes alle, and faste bynde,
> That from his bond no wight the wey out wiste;
> And hertes colde, hem wolde I that he twiste
> To make hem love, and that hem liste ay rewe
> On hertes sore, and kepe hem that ben trewe.

The first four lines of this stanza echo the wish expressed in the concluding sentence of the metrum (that the same bond of love that governs the universe might govern men's hearts), but the difference of wording, and context, leaves an uncertainty as to whether the 'love' that is to encircle all hearts with its bond is Divine Love or Cupid. The point the ambiguity is making, I think, is that Troilus is unaware of the difference. There is no reason to suspect his sincerity in praising the 'holy bond of love', and in one aspect it is not ironical that he should do so, not incon-gruous with the Boethian philosophy. When Philosophia said that it is good that men seek happiness in diverse ways, even in false goods, for it shows how great is the strength of nature, what she was referring to was the 'entencioun to comen to good', the natural impulse to seek the true happiness, which is the impulse of all love. Troilus hymn shows that what his love is really seeking is that good, the Love he praises in his hymn: the 'enten-cioun' to come to it is there, but it is blind to the extent that he can confuse the good with what can only be a false good in the terms of his own hymn. Philosophia had also said that even the false goods may give some inkling of the nature of the true good; and this, too, may be a (non-ironical) point that Chaucer is making, for example, in the last part of this final stanza. For love of any kind can 'twiste' cold hearts, and may keep them 'trewe' in the sense that love kept Troilus' heart true. But unless the 'trouthe' takes its impulse in the 'stable feyth' that directs love to its true end, the 'trouthe', like the love itself, will be wasted on a false good, and thus will be a perversion. The irony need not negate the 'idealism' of Troilus' attitude: he can mean all that he says, and what he says is true in itself in terms of the Boethian philosophy, and applicable in part to his own love—but not in the most important part. To give this hymn to Troilus is to reveal how misdirected is his love, since the very terms of the hymn make clear that the 'holy bond of love' must exclude a love that had become an end in itself.

The earlier reference to love as 'the holy bond of thynges' in Troilus' address of thanksgiving in the same book (1254-74) is in a context still more ambiguous—so ambiguous indeed as to explain why Chaucer felt it necessary to make the allusion clearer by inserting the later hymn to love. The address is spoken when Troilus finds himself at last in Criseyde's bed, and eventually in her arms, and it begins:

> O Love, O Charite,
> Thi moder ek, Citherea the swete,
> After thi self next heried be she,
> Venus mene I, the wel-willy planete . . .

No doubt Troilus thinks he is addressing Cupid and his mother Venus, and in this aspect the irony of the identification of Love with Charity is obvious. But the intention of the irony may not be so obvious; for when Troilus goes on to say that in praising Venus it is the 'wel-willy planete' he is referring to, he is, so to speak, justifying the identification of Love with Charity, if we think of the planet Venus as the agent of Divine Love. What the ambiguity reveals is, again, Troilus' confusion—his inability to distinguish between cupidinous love and charitable love. And there is a similar confusion when he goes on to include Hymen in his invocation: he is blind enough to regard his 'acord' with Criseyde as equivalent to marriage. The last two of the three stanzas of the address are an interesting example of the parodic language often used in the poem, where the terms of Christian worship are applied to the love situation:

> Benigne love, thow holy bond of thynges, (III. 1261)
> Whoso wol grace, and list the nought honouren,
> Lo, his desir wol fle withouten wynges.
> And noldestow of bounte hem socouren
> That serven best, and most alwey labouren,
> Yit were al lost, that dar I wel seyn, certes,
> But if thi grace passed oure desertes.

> And for thow me, that koude leest deserve
> Of hem that noumbred ben unto thi grace,
> Hast holpen, ther I likly was to sterve,
> And me bistowed in so heigh a place,
> That thilke boundes may no blisse pace,
> I kan no more; but laude and reverence
> Be to thy bounte and thyn excellence!

In the first of these stanzas Chaucer is giving to Troilus the beautiful words from Dante's *Paradiso* of a prayer to grant the pilgrim grace for the Beatific Vision;[1] and in transfer-ring the prayer to Troilus, he is transferring it to what, for Troilus, is a parallel situation, possibly with the hope that

[1] Canto 33. 13–18, cited by Root in his note to III. 1262–7.

the audience, or reader, would recognize the allusion and take the point. As Siegfried Wenzel observes, in both poems 'The "hero" is at the threshold of the climax of bliss. Yet what a difference in the kinds of bliss!'[1] Wenzel's view is that 'Such parodic passages—if they are to be considered as more than purple patches—do not necessarily debase the lovers' joy, but they certainly and unmistakably remind the audience of the existence of a higher love.' But the irony, or parody, of this passage surely does more than this; for the stanza is addressed to 'Benigne love, thow holy bond of thynges', and like his later hymn in praise of that Love, what it says is applicable to Troilus' own love in a way he is unaware of (if his love, or any love, wishes for grace without wishing to honour that Benign Love, it is trying to fly without wings). A medieval audience, less afraid than we are now to bring laughter near to holy things, would be quick to see the absurdity of the compari- son that Troilus' words invite, when he gives thanks to love for bestowing him in 'so heigh a place | That thilke boundes may no blisse pace'. It is true that if we read his words in the way he intends them we have what C. S. Lewis calls, with reference to similar parodic passages in the *De Amore* of Andreas Capellanus, 'a strange reduplica- tion of experience', which Lewis sees as part of the 'religion' of 'courtly love':[2] in every way Troilus' attitude follows correctly the attitude of Christian worship. But the very closeness of the parody betrays the irony: it becomes a travesty, an abuse of terms, in the circumstances of the address. As in his later hymn to love, there is no reason to doubt the sincerity of Troilus' idealistic attitude: what the parody is exposing is the absurdity of elevating sexual

---

[1] 'Chaucer's Troilus of Book IV', *PMLA* lxxix (1964), p. 547.
[2] *The Allegory of Love*, p. 42.

passion into a 'religion'. But how far Troilus himself is the
butt of the irony is another question. What confuses the
issue is the literary convention of French courtly romance
that allowed stories from antiquity to be used as vehicles for
medieval courtly sentiment and courtly behaviour, and the
convention of medieval love poetry in which religious and
erotic terms are interchangeable. For these conventions
together permit a lover, even in a story from ancient Troy,
to express himself both in the language of medieval
feudalism and in terms of Christian tradition—which may
give the impression that the pagan setting is irrelevant.
But in spite of the anachronisms of his narration Chaucer
clearly regards his hero as a pagan, as his epilogue proves.
And Christian doctrine itself recognizes that a pagan
without benefit of faith or grace is at the 'natural' stage:
strictly speaking he cannot be blamed for not knowing that
fornication is against the divine law. And it is possible
that this was in Chaucer's mind when he gave to Troilus
the words:

> And noldestow of bounte hem socouren
> That serven best, and most alwey labouren,
> Yit were al lost, that dar I wel seyn, certes,
> But if thi grace passed oure desertes.

For the only 'grace' that Troilus can know is the grace of
the gods he praises. This does not rob the words of their
ironic, moralistic significance, but it may mean that the
target of the irony is less Troilus himself than the literary
convention that made the 'reduplication of experience'
possible. Chaucer's use of the convention in this passage
reveals the conclusion to which the reduplication of
experience must, logically, lead. It is surely a *reductio ad
absurdum* to describe the lovers' bed as 'so heigh a place |
That thilke boundes may no blisse pace', in a context

which identifies the consummation of sexual passion with the Beatific Vision. That similar hyperbolic descriptions of lovers' joy became commonplaces of love poetry does not negate their possible ironic implications in poetry that has a moral significance.

If Troilus' love had been of the kind he praises in his hymns he would not have been subject by it, as he was, to Fortune's rule. When he learns that Criseyde must leave Troy he suffers intensely and blames Fortune for her injustice, since it is through no fault of his own that Criseyde must go, and he cannot understand how Fortune can treat him so cruelly when he has honoured her all his life (IV. 260–87). Pandarus, the philosopher, has a some-what clearer understanding of Fortune, but it does not go beyond Philosophia's 'lyghtere medicynes'—her defence of Fortune in Fortune's own terms, that is, as she operates in her own realm, incapable in her blindness of knowing her real function. When Troilus had first complained that Fortune was his foe (I. 837), Pandarus had replied in these terms: if her wheel should cease turning, she would cease to be Fortune, but just as her joys pass so do her sorrows, and so her very mutability should be ground for comfort (841–54). Yet when Troilus is at the height of his happiness, Pandarus tries to warn him to preserve it, with the argument:

> For of fortunes sharp adversitee   (III. 1625)
> The worste kynde of infortune is this:
> A man to han ben in prosperitee,
> And it remembren whan it passed is.

This is an echo of the complaint made by 'Boethius' (II, prosa 4), but the irony is that Pandarus' advice is futile—even though what he is warning Troilus about is what is to happen to him. For the happiness that is a gift of Fortune is in her hands to take away if she pleases. Only the happiness that comes from within is not subject to her rule, as Philosophia's reply to 'Boethius' explains. Later, when the news comes that Criseyde is to be sent away, Pandarus is momentarily shocked that Fortune should have over- thrown their happiness in so short a time, but adds sententiously:

> But who may al eschue, or al devyne?   (IV. 389)
> Swich is this world; forthi I thus deffyne,
> Ne trust no wight to fynden in Fortune
> Ay propretee: hire yiftes ben comune.

The last two lines are from Fortune's own argument (II, prosa 2) that what comes to men as her gift is not really theirs: it is hers to give as she pleases. Thus what Fortune gives is no man's 'propretee' for always: no one has the monopoly of her gifts.

These references to Fortune take their place as part of the characterization of Pandarus: they help to typify his philosophical attitude, his resourcefulness in finding a plausible explanation for everything. But there is irony in giving to the one who appoints himself as mentor in this way an understanding of Fortune that is incomplete. His 'who may al eschue or al devyne ?' is a hint that there is more to it; and his 'Swich is this world' defines the limitations of his arguments. For what he has to say applies to Fortune on the level of this world only. But as Philosophia explains in her 'strengere medicynes', all fortune is good, since it is Providence at the hub who turns Fortune's wheel. And the nearer to the hub of the wheel the less its motion is felt. Thus what we call bad fortune is good if we understand the providential purpose. In this way, Philosophia tells 'Boethius', 'it is set in your hand what fortune yow is levest. For alle fortune that semeth scharp or aspre, yif it ne exercise nat the goode folk ne chastiseth the wikkide folk, it punysseth' (IV, prosa 7). She says this in her 'lesson' that those who seek their happiness in gifts of fortune must suffer frustration, but that the frustration is itself a part of the providential order, and therefore good for them, if only they could realize it. Troilus has no Philosophia to teach him, only a Pandarus whose understanding is incomplete; and when he is to lose the happiness that he himself recognizes as a gift of fortune, he can only see the loss as an injustice. Chaucer's irony underlines Troilus' lack of understanding by stressing, more pointedly than Boccaccio had done, Troilus' subjection to Fortune and at the same time giving to him the hymn in praise of the divine order. For a love for a gift of fortune cannot belong to the 'holy bond of love'. It is because Troilus loves Criseyde for her 'persone' and not for her 'goodness', and because his love has become an idolatrous passion, that it keeps him at the rim of Fortune's wheel. If he had understood this, the loss of Criseyde could have chastised him: he does not understand, and so Fortune is able to punish him. The poet's own ironic interventions in the form of apostrophe and lyrical comment help to stress the point—as at the beginning of the Proem to the fourth book:

> But al to litel, weylawey the whyle,
> Lasteth swich joie, ythonked be Fortune,
> That semeth trewest whan she wol bygyle,
> And kan to fooles so hire song entune,
> That she hem hent and blent, traitour comune.

The longest Boethian paraphrase in the poem is, like Troilus' hymn to love, a passage which Chaucer almost

certainly inserted in a revision of the poem[1]—Troilus'
speech on the problem of reconciling God's foreknowledge with man's free will, spoken in the temple where he
has gone to pray for death in his anguish at the thought of
losing Criseyde (IV. 958–1078). It is a summary of the
first part of the arguments 'Boethius' uses when he is
seeking enlightenment on the subject. 'Boethius' finds it
difficult to understand how, if God foreknows our actions,
those actions can come from our free will to act. For if
God's foreknowledge is perfect, we can only do or think
what he has already foreseen; and to ascribe to him imperfect knowledge is 'felonye and unleveful'. There are
some who say that God's foreknowledge does not cause
things to happen, but that he foresees them because they
are going to happen, but this seems to 'Boethius' only
changing things round without altering the quality of
necessity imposed on everything that happens if it is foreseen: if it is foreseen it *must* happen, just as when we see a
man sitting on a seat he must be sitting, since if he is
sitting our opinion that he is sitting must be true, and if it is
true he must necessarily be sitting. So the quality of necessity is in both the sitting and the truth. And this example
seems to him to illustrate his problem, that whether things
to come are foreseen by God or whether the things foreseen by him are to come, there can be no freedom of
choice. But this conclusion troubles him, since if there is
no freedom of will for man, 'thanne ne sculle ther nevere
be, ne nevere were, vice ne vertu', and—even more
'felonous' and more 'wikke'—it follows that, since this
ordering of things comes from God, then 'oure vices ben
referrid to the makere of alle good' (V, prosa 3). This then
is the dilemma he puts to Philosophia, and she answers

---

[1] See R. K. Root, *Textual Tradition*, pp. 216–20.

him with the argument that when God foresees free acts, he foresees them as free, and the foreseeing does not make them less free, since God, being eternal, lives in a perpetual present, while the world operates only in time, so that what we regard as 'before' and 'after' is always 'now' to him. He does not foresee, he simply sees; and just as when we see the sun rising, our seeing does not cause it to rise, or when we see a man walking, our seeing him walk does not cause him to walk, so God's seeing does not detract from the freedom of what he (fore)sees. He sees the necessary as necessary and the free as free, and the view that he has of our future free acts does not make them necessary.

Troilus' long speech follows 'Boethius' up to the point where he had concluded that, whichever way we look at it, God's foreknowledge must preclude freedom of will. In its length, and from its very nature, the speech seems inept, dramatically and poetically. We might think of Romeo's reaction, in a parallel situation, when, offered 'Adversity's sweet milk, philosophy', he cries, 'Hang up philosophy, unless philosophy can make a Juliet'. Although dramatic propriety seems to have counted less with Chaucer than his *sentence*, this is among the worst instances of his disregard of it, and he must have had his reasons for using such intractable material. No doubt the main reason was its relevance to Troilus' attitude, for Troilus unlike 'Boethius' is not dismayed that the conclusion of his arguments must be to relieve man of the responsibility of his actions. And we can appreciate the irony of Troilus' 'proof' that 'al that comth comth of necessitee', used to support a decision already taken by him, of his own volition, not to take any action to prevent Criseyde's departure—'Thus to be lorn, it is my destinee'.[1] There is irony also in the fact that the Boethian arguments he uses were in reality intended only as a state~ ment of the problem by 'Boethius' and to be refuted later. And there may have been other reasons which led Chaucer to make the speech so long (and so tedious). The tone of mockery in the reference to 'some | That han hire top ful heighe and smothe yshore' (995-6) is like the mocking tone taken to the same philosophical problem in the *Nun's Priest's Tale*, when Chaunticleer remarks:

> That in scole is greet altercacioun (3237)
> In this mateere, and greet disputisoun,
> And hath been of an hundred thousand men.

It looks as though Chaucer found somewhat ludicrous the protracted scholastic debate on the question, and perhaps he saw in the dialectic of 'Boethius' an opportunity for parody. For there is something absurd in the way that 'Boethius' labours through all the learned theories, when the conclusion he reaches is, after all, one that he himself cannot accept; and his reasoning will not stand up to scrutiny, as Philosophia shows, for example, in his analogy of the man sitting on a seat. In Troilus' long speech, I think Chaucer is parodying, by a slight exaggeration, both the methods of reasoning used by 'Boethius' and his heavy hand. For example:

> For if ther sit a man yond on a see, (IV. 1023)
> Than by necessite bihoveth it
> That, certes, thyn opynyoun sooth be,
> That wenest, or conjectest, that he sit;

---

[1] Charles A. Owen, jun. writes: 'The irony of Troilus' coming to a decision through a train of thought that rejects freedom of the will was perhaps no small part of the passage's appeal to Chaucer', 'The Significance of Chaucer's Revisions of *Troilus and Criseyde*', MP lv (1957), p. 4.

And further overe now ayeinward yit,
Lo, right so is it of the part contrarie,
As thus—nowe herkne, for I wol nat tarie—. . .

And the joke of it is that the conclusion that Troilus reaches with such obvious effort is the one that in the *Consolation* is proved to have been reached by false reasoning.

Thus Chaucer is doing here exactly what he did with the earlier Boethian topics—using Boethian arguments, recognizably but speciously, to reach a conclusion different from that to which those arguments led ultimately in the *Consolation*. And like Criseyde's speech on 'fals felicitee', this one is consistent with the character of the person who speaks it. Troilus regards what happens to him always as coming from outside—from the inescapable power of the god of love, from Fortune, from 'necessitee', never from his own volition. In inserting this speech for Troilus, then, Chaucer rounded off a process already begun. He had used the first two of the three topics of the *Consolation*, mainly in the mouths of Pandarus and Criseyde; Troilus' speech deals with the third and final topic by the same method. The symmetry achieved by the completion of the process is not an architectural symmetry: Chaucer was not so concerned as many medieval artists were with formal design. It is the more subtle kind of symmetry of *sentence* that he loved, especially when it involves irony of the 'upsodoun' kind that here gives to Pandarus, the philosopher, a philosophy of Fortune that leaves out the most important part; to Criseyde, the type of human falsity in love, a proof of the falsity of worldly happiness; and to Troilus a proof that man's will is not free, where the irony is that it is just because man's will is free that he may lose his freedom, as Troilus lost his.

Chaucer underlines this point in the description of the beginnings of Troilus' love for Criseyde. When he is reflecting on the image of her that he sees in the 'mirour of his mynde',

> he gan fully assente (1. 391)
> Criseyde for to love, and nought repente.

And in his song about love he asks:

> How may of the in me swich quantite, (1. 412)
> But if that I consente that it be?

But what he consents to is no freedom, for love 'held hym as his thral' (1. 439).

In keeping with the sustained irony of his narration, however, Chaucer appears to accept Troilus' view that what happens is only the operation of Destiny; many of the astrological references in the poem seem designed to this end. But these, too, must be approached with caution. W. C. Curry maintains that Troilus' view that 'al that comth comth of necessitee' is true of the whole narrative, by including among the deterministic factors what he calls 'Nature-as-Destiny'.[1] Such a term, however, can only be confusing. It is true that Curry's explanation of Destiny follows that of Boethius: as the figure of Fortune's wheel is designed to illustrate, Providence is the Divine Intelligence that comprehends in itself all the things of the world, their natures, and the laws of their development; in so far as it is unified in the Divine Intelligence the universal order is Providence, in so far as it is fragmented and incorporated in the things it rules it becomes what 'was of olde men clepyd destine'. But there is no place in Boethian philosophy for any concept of Destiny that would preclude man's free will. When God created man and gave him

---

[1] *Chaucer and the Medieval Sciences* (2nd edn. London, 1960), pp. 244 ff.

his place in the universal order, he created him with reason as an essential part of his nature, and as Philosophia says:

ther ne was nevere no nature of resoun that it ne hadde liberte of fre wil. For every thing that may naturely usen resoun, it hath doom by which it discernith and demeth every thing; thanne knoweth it by itself thinges that ben to fleen and thinges that ben to desiren ... Wherfore in alle thingis that resoun is, in hem also is liberte of willynge and of nillynge (v, prosa 2)

Man's free will, which in this way is a necessary adjunct to the reason implanted in him by God, is therefore a part of the universal order of causes which is fixed for God and contained in his foreknowledge, but that does not destroy the freedom: God's foreknowledge is one and the same as his providence; in providing for man's freedom he founds it, not destroys it.[1]

The astrological influences which may affect men's physical characters and the course of their lives are also part of the order of causes that is fixed for God, and when Chaucer refers to astrological influences in his story he is reflecting the general medieval belief, held by philosophers and theologians alike, in a universal astrological determinism; but man's free will was always excluded from the scope of this determinism. Modern psychology of course would find it difficult to separate the will from 'character' in this way, but to the medieval mind character was more a physical concept than it is now (except perhaps to some doctors and chemical biologists), and the human will a moral concept, as the adjunct of reason. We are told in the second book that Venus 'nas not al a foo' to Troilus at his nativity, and, as Curry explains,

it is the province of Venus to bestow upon her children

[1] See Étienne Gilson, *L'Esprit de la philosophie médiévale* (Paris, 1932), chapitre v.

beautiful and elegantly formed bodies, together with characters inclined to luxuriousness and passionate love, but withal
upright and honorable. Though voluptuous and tempera-
mental by nature, the children of Venus possess a fine sense of
duty, a ready faith, great refinement, good breeding, delicacy of
feeling and kindliness of heart. They easily become leaders and
perform whatever they undertake with facility. They are given
to games, to laughter, to joyous living, rejoicing in the com-
panionship of friends, and relying upon others to the point of
being often deceived.[1]

'Viewed in this way, Troilus' 'nature' might be seen as
destined, but of course what are described here are potentialities only, and like Venus herself they are ambivalent.
It still lies with a person's reason and will, if he is a child
of Venus, to determine whether the voluptuousness will
prevail over the sense of duty, whether the reliance on
friends will lead astray.

Similarly destiny in the form of astrological influence
on events must be seen in relation to, and not as excluding,
the freedom of choice of the persons in Chaucer's story.
When the Moon is together with Saturn and Jove in
the sign of Cancer on the night when Criseyde goes to
Pandarus' house, the conjunction causes such a rain to
fall that all the women are afraid; and the time comes
for Criseyde to leave—

> But O, Fortune, executrice of wyerdes, (III. 617)
> O influences of thise hevenes hye,
> Soth is that, under god, ye ben our hierdes,
> Though to us bestes ben the causes wrie.
> This mene I now, for she gan homward hye,
> But execut was al bisyde hire leve
> The goddes wil, for which she moste bleve.

[1] *Chaucer and the Medieval Sciences*, p. 257.

This is Destiny, operating through the stars, and it is consistent with the attitude of Chaucer's narrator that he makes the most of it. But if Chaucer had really intended us to believe that Criseyde was the helpless victim of Fortune and the stars, would he have raised the question whether or not she was deceived by Pandarus into going to his house in the first place? When she asked if Troilus was there, Pandarus 'swor hire nay, for he was out of towne'; but he followed up his lie with protestations that, to the wary Criseyde who had already been tricked by him once into a meeting with Troilus, and who knew that Pandarus was intending to arrange a meeting at his house, should have been hint enough:

> nece, I pose that he were,　　　(III. 571)
> Yow thurste nevere han the more fere;
> For rather than men sholde hym ther aspie
> Me were levere a thousand fold to dye.

Since this whole scene is Chaucer's invention, the narrator's comment which follows—

> Nat list myn auctour fully to declare
> What that she thoughte whan he seyde so,
> That Troilus was out of towne yfare,
> As if he seyde soth therof or no. . . .—

must surely be the ironist's way of sowing the seeds of doubt. And when Criseyde herself goes on to beg Pandarus 'to be war of goosissh poeples speche' and be careful whom he brought there, the doubt must be strengthened; her concluding words, 'em, syn I most on yow triste, | Loke al be wel, for I do as yow liste' have a masterly ambiguity. She behaves of course with perfect decorum, and when the time comes is prepared to leave and only prevented from doing so by the rain, but the crucial decision was when she consented to go there in the first place, for all her suspicion.

We must beware then of taking too seriously the (perhaps suspiciously emphatic) insistence on the part played by Destiny in the story. Undoubtedly Fortune and the stars play their part, but more to work out a train of consequences initiated in the first place by a free choice made by the persons concerned. But as Philosophia explains, the souls of men are less free when they are in the bodies, and this, too, Chaucer recognizes in recognizing the power of the goddess Venus. But it is only when sexual desire becomes passion that freedom is totally lost, for

the last servage is whan that thei [the souls] ben yeven to vices and han ifalle fro the possessioun of hire propre resoun. For aftir that thei han cast awey hir eyghen fro the lyght of the soverayn sothfastnesse to lowe thingis and derke, anon thei derken by the cloude of ignoraunce and ben troubled by felonous talentz; to the whiche talentz whan thei approchen and assenten, thei hepen and encrecen the servage which thei hepen and encrecen the servage which thei han joyned to hemself; and in this manere thei ben caytifs fro hir propre liberte (v, prosa 2).

As we shall see later, these images of light/dark/cloud are images that Chaucer uses in his poem, and help to provide the clues to the ambiguities of some of the key passages.

Many critics have seen in the poem the Boethian pattern of Fortune and Providence while still maintaining that it is only its mutability that distinguishes the lovers' happiness from true happiness: they usually find two levels of meaning, the celebration of the love happiness being the prime concern of the first part of the story, and its mutability being the 'moralitee'. The fact that it is a love outside marriage is awkward, but the awkwardness is got round in various ways—by the neither entirely true nor entirely logical argument that in Chaucer's day the aristocracy could not marry for love, hence 'it would have been irrelevant to talk about marriage in this connection'[1], or by the more cautious, but no more convincing argument:

[Chaucer] takes what we can now see to be the simplest and most obvious course—he merely says that these matters are ordered differently elsewhere [referring to the Proem to Book II] . . . [he also] deals with his problem mainly by silence . . . Of course he was helped in his silence about marriage by the fact that he was writing in a tradition which had often dis-sociated love and marriage.[2]

But Chaucer's silence about marriage is of a kind that implicitly raises the question of the illicitness of the love. When Troilus in his hymn to love substitutes for the reference to the 'sacrament of mariages of chaste loves', in the original, the less precise 'couples doth in vertu for to dwelle', the evasion must have an ironic force, since, even if there could be any question of an illicit love being regarded in a medieval context as 'dwelling in virtue', it is not the kind of bond that could be comprehended in the terms of the hymn. Those familiar with the Boethian original, or with the Christian doctrine it formulates, must recognize the evasion, and take the ironic point that, even with its help Troilus is condemning his own 'acord' with Criseyde out of his own mouth.

There is a further difficulty for those critics who leap this hurdle of the marriage question too lightly. If the love

[1] Dorothy Bethurum, 'Chaucer's Point of View as Narrator in the Love Poems', *PMLA*, lxxiv, N.S. lxvii (1959), p. 519.

[2] D. S. Brewer, 'Love and Marriage in Chaucer's Poetry', *MLR* xlix (1954), p. 463.

in the story is 'separated by only the thinnest partition' from lawful love, what is it that Chaucer is warning his 'yonge, fresshe folkes' against in the epilogue? This is where mutability comes to the rescue. Dorothy Bethurum writes:

If Troilus and Criseyde are illustrations of love's power, their short happiness is also an illustration of the mutability that marks all earthly life. Not for nothing did Chaucer give them their universal role. Hence the ending of the poem. Chaucer's pity and irony join in his wish to spare the 'yonge fresshe folk' love's sorrow, but he knows nevertheless that 'may no man fordo the lawe of kynde'. If one could love God solely he would never know Troilus' sorrow, but for most youth on this earth that is not a possibility. Nor is it desirable, if the human race is to continue.[1]

This is an interpretation based on a misreading of which many have been guilty: nowhere does Chaucer say, ironically or otherwise, that young folk to avoid Troilus' sorrow should love God 'solely', and he never suggests that they should deny or suppress their love. He admonishes them to repair 'home' from worldly vanity,[2] and to look up to God who made them in his image,

and thynketh al nys but a faire   (v. 1840)
This world, that passeth soone as floures faire.

These lines express, as only great poetry can express complex

[1] 'Chaucer's Point of View as Narrator in the Love Poems', p. 518.
[2] Cf. Chaucer's *Balade de Bon Conseil, Truth*:

Her is noon hoom, her nis but wildernesse: (17)
Forth, pilgrim forth! Forth, beste, out of thy stal!
Know thy contree, look up, thank God of al;
Holde the heye wey, and lat thy gost thee lede;
And trouthe thee shal delivere, it is no drede.

He uses 'trouthe' here in its more spiritual sense, the equivalent of the 'stable feyth' referred to above.

meaning briefly in imagery, the whole paradoxical
doctrine that while the world and all it holds is beautiful
and good in itself, it can become bad (for us) if we do not
recognize where our true home is. Hence the ambiguity
of the word 'faire'. In one sense it has the meaning it has,
for example, in Gower's 'For al is bot a chirie feire | This
worldes good',[1] but a 'faire' is also a beautiful thing, and,
in still another sense, an affair or activity. And all these
senses are relevant in the context here. For as a beautiful
thing, the world passes soon 'as floures faire', and so its
beauty is deceptive,[2] and as 'affairs', the things of this
world assume too great an importance if we forget how
transitory they are.[3] It is true that the philosophy of life
that this complex of ideas expresses is a philosophy that,
pushed to its logical extremity, had been held to imply
that it is only by complete detachment from the world that
man can attain, as near as it is possible in this world, to
complete happiness (in contemplation of the Supreme
Good, which is his 'home'). But the medieval doctrine
which defined the philosophy for Christians did not
suggest that this is the only way to find true happiness;
nor does Chaucer suggest to his 'yonge, fresshe folkes'
that it is. To 'repeyre hom fro worldly vanite' is not
necessarily to turn one's back on the world: it is to realize
its transitory nature and the relative unimportance of its
affairs; it is to see the beauty of the world as the work of its
Creator, and not prize it only for its own sake; it is to love
in the world only what is good, for in loving for the sake

[1] *Confessio Amantis*, Prol. 454–5.
[2] 'In a toumbe is al the faire above, And under is the corps' (*Squire's Tale*
518).
[3] 'Ne þenk þu nevere | þi lif to narruliche leden | ne þine faires | to faste
holden' (*Proverbs of Alfred*, 518–21).

of the goodness we are also loving God, whether we know it or not. We were given the power to turn our hearts to God in this way when we were created in his image, but through our own weakness it is a power that needs now the help of God's grace. And so Chaucer exhorts his young people to love him, who, 'right for love', died on the Cross to redeem our souls:

> For he nyl falsen no wight, dar I seye, (1845)
> That wol his herte al holly on hym leye.
> And syn he best to love is, and most meke,
> What nedeth feyned loves for to seke?

To set one's heart wholly on Christ is not to love him 'solely': that would be contrary to his fundamental teaching. Love of God does not exclude love of his creatures, but it does exclude 'feyned loves', that is, loves that are conceived or believed in erroneously[1]—in Boethian terms, loves of a 'false good'.

This 'moralitee' explicit in the epilogue is implicit in the ironies of the narrative. It is not only the mutability that is attached to all earthly things that the story illustrates. For those who have set their hearts wholly on God the mutability can be accepted as part of the divine purpose. When death has freed Troilus from his blind submission to Fortune's dominion, he too can look down on this little earth and laugh to see the sorrow of 'hem that wepte for his deth so faste'. And in the following stanza Chaucer sums up the Boethian *sentence* of his story—'Swich fyn hath, lo, this Troilus for love! | Swich fyn hath al his grete worthynesse! . . .'. Such is the end that Troilus has for love—a 'feyned love' in the Boethian terms in which the poet has presented it. The fact that, in strict truth, Troilus did not

---

[1] See *OED*, s.v. Feign, sense 4 b.

die 'for love' does not really matter, for there is a sense in which the words are true:

> From hennesforth, as ferforth as I may,   (v. 1717)
> Myn owen deth in armes wol I seche;
> I recche nat how soone be the day.

Such is the end also of his 'grete worthinesse', his superior royal rank, and his 'noblesse'. These are things which were, or could have been, good. But, as Philosophia explained, all mortals are of noble seed, and no man is 'ongentil' unless he encourages his heart to abuse this 'gentilesse' of his birth (III, metrum 6). As a royal prince, however, Troilus had special obligations which he dishonoured when he resigned his 'estat roial' into Criseyde's hands at the very outset of his love. At first this 'love service' seems to have an ennobling effect, in that he acquits himself more bravely in battle because of it, and

> bicome the frendlieste wight,   (I. 1079)
> The gentileste, and ek the moste fre,
> The thriftieste, and oon the beste knyght
> That in his tyme was, or myghte be;
> Dede were his japes and his cruelte,
> His hye port, and his manere estraunge;
> And ech of tho gan for a vertu chaunge.

But just what the transformation amounted to is seen when Criseyde has to leave Troy. He is ready to abscond with her, without a thought for the defence of Troy, and it is not his 'noblesse', but his lady's wish, that deters him.[1] And when she has gone he takes to his bed with grief, so that Pandarus has to rouse him with the reminder that folk will say he is pretending to be sick 'for cowardise' (v. 412). The parallel with what happened before he won Criseyde

[1] See Alan T. Gaylord, '*Gentilesse* in Chaucer's *Troilus*', *SP* lxi (1964), p. 31.

is clear. When love made him braver in battle, it was not 'for the rescous of the town', but only 'To liken hire the bet for his renoun' (1. 477–81). And when Pandarus found him bewailing in his room alone, it was by taunting him with fear of the Greeks that he roused him (1. 553–60). The ennobling effect of love clearly has its limitations.

Such is the end also, the stanza of the epilogue tells us, of 'false worldes brotelnesse', which includes both the 'brotelnesse' of a false Criseyde and that of a world false because it seems to hold out a promise of a stable happiness which it cannot keep. But to see the 'brotelnesse' and falseness of the world in terms only of mutability is to miss the point of the Boethian concept of Fortune and her wheel. The last two lines of the stanza—'And thus bigan his lovyng of Criseyde, | As I have told, and in this wise he deyde'—to E. Talbot Donaldson 'seem to express a deep sadness for a doomed potential',[1] and this is how we must see them if we have failed to perceive the relation between cause and effect that the lines imply, and that the ironies of the narrative have revealed. If we perceive that relation the sadness must be for a wasted, rather than a doomed, potential. It all began with Troilus' loving of Criseyde in the way the poet has told, and this is how it ended—in his death and the end of all his 'grete worthynesse'. It is worthy to be true in love as he was to Criseyde, but it is a waste and a perversion of such 'trouthe' to use it in the service of a false good. As in his love, so in his worthiness there was great potentiality, but it too came to nothing because, like his love, it was misdirected by sexual passion.

But Troilus had his punishment here on earth, through this 'false worldes brotelnesse' itself, and since his 'wo in

[1] 'The Ending of Chaucer's *Troilus*' p. 41.

lovynge of Criseyde' was through his blindness, we are not
invited to judge him further. It matters little whether the
eighth sphere to which he was taken was the sphere of the
moon or the *stellatum*, for his translation there was only to
give him an enlightened view of this little earth below,
before he went forth to where 'Mercurye sorted hym to
dwelle'. The address to 'yonge, fresshe folkes' that follows
the conclusion of the narrative is a clear statement for
Christians that sexual love need not deflect them from the
way to true happiness as it had deflected Troilus. For
Troilus was not a Christian, as the next stanza reminds us:

> Lo here, of payens corsed olde rites!   (v. 1849)
> Lo here, what alle hire goddes may availle!
> Lo here, thise wrecched worldes appetites!
> Lo here, the fyn and guerdoun for travaille
> Of Jove, Appollo, of Mars, of swich rascaille!
> Lo here, the forme of olde clerkes speche
> In poetrie, if ye hire bokes seche!

This stanza 'places' Troilus for us in relation to the Christian
doctrine of love defined in the preceding stanzas, and I
think helps to explain Chaucer's attitude to his story in
relation to the Boethian ideas he introduces into it. The
point of the *Consolation of Philosophy* had been to demonstrate, whether or not it entirely succeeds, that the conclusions it reaches can be reached in the light of philosophy
itself, by stages of reasoning independent of 'resouns ytaken
fro withouten'—in other words, that they are absolute
truths. When Chaucer takes his pagan story from the
'olde clerkes', and gives to the persons in it arguments or
passages from the *Consolation* that apply to their own
situations or attitudes in ways they did not intend, he is, in
a way, endorsing what the *Consolation* was trying to prove
—that the arguments apply in an absolute sense, if we

accept the premisses. The problem of love his poem is concerned with is a universal problem which medieval Christian doctrine and philosophy tried to solve, not a problem created by that doctrine and inherent only in it. Even a modern humanist can appreciate the truths that Chaucer's story exemplifies—that a happiness that depends on externals (the gifts of fortune) is at best a deceptive happiness, and that a sexual love which may feel itself in the beginning to be an ennobling and uplifting force may either prove to be unstable or turn into a stultifying passion, deadening to everything but itself, unless there is some reason greater than physical desire for the love; though a humanist, of course, would not accept the solution in the Christian form in which Chaucer puts it in his epilogue. And it is this Christian solution that is implicit in the ironies of the narrative, as well as the problem itself. Yet if we judge Troilus in the light of the Christian morality that is offered to the reader, I think we are seeing him in too harsh a light. It is one thing for Troilus in his blindness to use the words of a prayer to the Virgin as he lies in his mistress's bed, and to refer to the consummation of his sexual passion in terms of the Beatific Vision—but for a Christian hero to do so would be revolting. What makes possible the comedy, and the lightness of touch of the wit, is that the Christian allusions in Troilus' words do not mean to him what they mean to the reader—hence the irony.

There is still the question of the 'lawe of kynde', which Chaucer mentions in his own ambiguous way, and which is, I think, central to his meaning. But this belongs to another chapter. For it would be misleading to treat all the ambiguities of the poem under the Boethian heading, even when they have relevance to the ideas expressed in the *Consolation*. Already, by the isolation of the Boethian paraphrases there has been, inevitably, a distortion, a too narrow view of the poem. A poet does not write like a philosopher: what philosophy his poem is expressing becomes a part of a homogeneous whole that is the poem; and though we may look for its message in its philosophical or social relevance, we would be unwise to assume that this is the *raison d'être* of the poem. In *Troilus* the emotional effect of the poetry, the comedy, and the wit are important factors in the total effect; and while it is true that these are inseparable from its moralistic relevance, who could say whether Chaucer wrote the poem in the way he did because he saw in the story an opportunity to illustrate ironically the Boethian topics, or whether he saw in the Boethian topics an opportunity to tell his story in these witty terms? All we can say from the evidence of the poem itself is that he saw in Boccaccio's poem in relation to the Boethian philosophy the possibilities for the complex poem he makes of it. Critical analysis can never do full justice to that complexity, since it is forced to separate elements that are themselves a part of the compound of the poetry, and that take their full meaning from being a part of the compound, especially in the more poetic passages. But analysis can help, in its own heavy-footed way, if it draws attention to the elements of the compound; and its very prolixity can serve, by contrast, to show up the economy and wit of the original.

CHAPTER III

Ambiguity and the Narrator

THERE are at least two ways in which we can see the narrator in *Troilus and Criseyde*, and both are useful to describe the part he plays in the total effect of the poem. To see him as a fictional character makes it easier to accept that the attitude of apparent approval of the love story in the first three books need not be taken at its face value, and at the same time helps to explain how the irony is made to work without destroying the sympathy with the persons in the story. The very personal nature of the narration is a vital element in the poem's artistic success: it is because we have been made to feel the narrator's constant presence and active involvement throughout the narrative that the address to 'yonge, fresshe folkes' at the end can come with the naturalness and warmth of a human appeal, and not as an abstract 'moralitee'. On this level—seen wholly as a *persona* distinct from the poet—the narrator becomes a kind of 'Boethius', whose unseeing eye is brought gradually to a clearer vision as the story proceeds to its inevitable end. Charles Muscatine, for example, writes of him:

But toward the end of the story, as if belatedly learning from it, he draws back from the action and more into our line of vision. He becomes a storyteller again. He depends more on his 'olde bokes'. He is now less an occasional victim of irony than, with us, a perceiver of it. There creeps into his still active sympathy a note of detachment: . . . Then, moved by Troilus' fate, and as if to compensate for the recency of his discovery of the story's meaning, he steps right before us and announces it in the epilogue, with triumphant rhetoric and movingly eloquent exhortation.[1]

There is another aspect of the narrator's function, however, which this view of him as a wholly fictional character may tend to obscure, and that is his function as a vehicle for the wit by which the poet expresses his own commentary in the ironic ambiguities, especially of his interventions in the narrative. It is this aspect that Robert Payne is referring to when he defines the difference between Boccaccio and Chaucer, as narrators of the same story, in these words:

[Boccaccio] continues to weave into and around the narrative a ground of expressive and evaluative language which makes of the whole a sustained personal lyric. Chaucer intrudes upon the action of his poem for exactly opposite reasons: to remain constantly between the reader and the action, objectifying it for him and eliciting from him an attitude toward it.[2]

This comment does not conflict with the view of the narrator as a fictional character, but it puts its finger on his real function in the poem. The interventions come at each important stage in the narrative and serve to direct attention to what is the focal point of that part of the story with relevance to its *sentence*. And in the first three books they 'elicit an attitude' from the reader by their ambiguity, ostensibly putting one point of view, but in an ambivalent form of expression. In the last two books, however, when the lovers' happiness is ended abruptly, the ambivalence is no longer so necessary: the poet, who till now has spoken with a double voice, can take over the narrative more

---

[1] *Chaucer and the French Tradition*, p. 161.
[2] *The Key of Remembrance*, pp. 176–7.

directly and speak with his own voice, ironic at times but less ambiguously so, less at the expense of the narrator. Significantly perhaps, there are few interventions in the fourth book, which relates how the separation of the lovers was effected and has therefore less in the action that is of direct moralistic relevance than the earlier books. This is not to say, however, that the attitudes the interventions elicit from the reader are necessarily moralistic attitudes. In the last two books especially they are often to enlist our sympathy, and even to discourage us from passing judge- ment.

When Payne observed that the role Chaucer creates for his narrator almost necessarily implies a complementary role for the audience, he was referring in particular to the 'self-deprecatory ironies'. But in the narrator's first major intervention in the story there is another way in which his direct address to the audience becomes a way of involving the reader, when, in holding Troilus up as a warning to the audience not to scorn love, his words have an ambi- guity that gives them a wider, and more complex applica- bility. The more obvious reference of the words serves to give the poet a greater freedom to express his complex meaning than he need appear to be using. The interven- tion comes at the point where Troilus in the temple has been speaking scornfully of lovers:

> At which the god of love gan loken rowe   (1. 206)
> Right for despit, and shop for to be wroken;
> He kidde anon his bowe nas nat broken;
> For sodeynly he hitte hym atte fulle,
> And yit as proud a pekok kan he pulle.

P. M. Kean has shown, in an analysis of this and the stanzas immediately following, that these lines correspond to the second part of stanza 25 of the first book of *Il*

Filostrato, which follows Troilo's mockery of lovers and his declaration of his intention not to fall himself into the snare again. Before Troilo leaves the temple he is to become once more the victim of love, so his 'intention' is contra-dicted by the event, and the first part of Boccaccio's stanza, which reads (in the translation cited by Miss Kean), 'O blindness of mundane minds! How often follow effects all contrary to our intentions', obviously refers to this. Chaucer transposes this first part of the stanza, putting it, with a slight but significant difference of wording, *after* the mention of the god of love, and using it to introduce a passage of seven stanzas of commentary beginning:

> O blynde world, O blynde entencioun!   (I. 211)
> How often falleth al the effect contraire
> Of surquidrie, and foule presumpcioun;
> For kaught is proud, and kaught is debonaire.
> This Troilus is clomben on the staire,
> And litel weneth that he moot descenden;
> But al day faileth thing that fooles wenden.

As Miss Kean points out, Chaucer's transposition of the comment, and his change of wording, enable him to give the comment a wider application than it had in *Il Filo-strato*, enable him to use it to introduce the idea of 'the inevitability of the descent from good to ill fortune . . . which applies to all human affairs and to the whole pattern of the tragedy which lies ahead'. Miss Kean adds, however:

Chaucer goes on to give another reason for the inevitability of the way in which Troilus's story develops. Love itself is part of the direction which Nature, by her laws, gives to all living beings. The point of the Bayard simile [in the next stanza] is that the horse that 'ginneth for to skippe *Out of the weye*' is forced to realize:

'Yit am I but an hors, *and horses lawe*
I moot endure, and with my feres draw.' (223–4)

Applied to Troilus 'this fierse and proude knyght' the simile
teaches us that:

> evere it was, and evere it shal byfalle,
> That love is he that alle thing may bynde;
> For may no man fordo the lawe of kynde. (236–8)[1]

Yet there is much in the whole of this intervention
by the narrator to suggest that it is not quite as simple as
this. D. W. Robertson, for example, claims that the
'horse' is a common symbol of fleshly appetite in medieval
literature and art,[2] and sees in the Bayard analogy a
moralistic irony: 'Just as a horse must obey "horses lawe",
so Troilus will succumb to the "lawe of kynde" which
dominates the fleshly or "horsy" aspect of man'.[3] But this
in turn can hardly be the whole meaning. The 'horses
lawe' which Bayard must endure is the control of the
whip, so if the 'horse' signifies fleshly appetite the analogy
should signify the control of fleshly appetite (by Reason).
And indeed it is probably the concept of the whip, or
bridle, that gave to the 'horse' its iconographic significance.
The obvious parallel between 'horses lawe' and the 'lawe
of kynde' is clearly not so straightforward as it might seem,
and with the help of Miss Kean's analysis of this passage
we can see perhaps a little further into what Chaucer is
doing exactly in this intervention. As she shows, he uses
it as a kind of full stop to the first part of the narrative, the
account of Troilus' scorn of lovers and the anger of the
god of love; but the statement 'sodeynly he hitte hym atte

---

[1] 'Chaucer's Dealings with a Stanza of *Il Filostrato,* etc.', pp. 38–9.
[2] See *Preface*, pp. 30, 194, 253–5, 394; and plates 6, 7, 8, 63, etc.
[3] *Preface*, p. 476.

fulle' serves both to conclude that part and to anticipate the second part of the narrative, which is resumed, after the intervention, at the point where Troilus is about to set eyes on Criseyde. This manœuvre serves to give greater weight to the intervention, as Miss Kean observes, by giving it a wider relevance, and so transforming it from the mere passing comment that it was in Boccaccio's poem. But it should be noticed that it also produces a rather curious disorder in the narrative which serves to give an ambivalence to what is said in the intervention: it can refer both backwards to Troilus' scorn of lovers and for/ wards to his own subjection to love. And it is this ambi/ valence, specifically, that gives the ambiguity, for example, to lines 215–16: the 'staire' on which Troilus has climbed becomes both his assumption of superiority to lovers and his later exaltation in his own love. And the same ambi/ valence operates in the Bayard analogy in the next stanza: in the backward view it refers to Troilus' scorn of lovers (the 'feres' with whom he refused to draw); in the forward view, as it refers to Troilus' subjection to the god of love, the horse that 'gynneth for to skippe | Out of the wey, so pryketh hym his corn' becomes sexual desire (the arrows of the god of love) which can lead astray ('Out of the wey') unless it is controlled by 'a lassh of the longe whippe' and taught that it must draw with its 'feres', that is, in harness with the other faculties or impulses. Thus the 'horses lawe' applies to Troilus in two ways—as the 'lawe' of sexual desire it applies as it is applied to him directly in the following stanza, to his fall from pride and subjection to the god of love, but it also applies to him ironically, as the ambiguity of the next stanza makes clear. It is in this stanza that the narrator turns to address the audience:

Forthy, ensample taketh of this man,   (1. 232)
Ye wise, proude, and worthi folkes alle,
To scornen love, which that so sone kan
The fredom of youre hertes to hym thralle;
For evere it was, and evere it shal byfalle,
That love is he that alle thing may bynde;
For may no man fordo the lawe of kynde.

In one meaning, coming as it does immediately after the
statement of Troilus' fall from pride and subjection to the
god of love, this is a warning not to scorn love as he had
scorned it. But there is an imprecision in the syntax of the
first sentence,[1] and the stanza could equally well be saying:
'Therefore take warning from this man, all you wise,
proud, and noble folk, to scorn love [of the kind] which
can so easily enslave to itself the freedom of your hearts;
for it always was, and always will be so, that love is he
[He] that can bind all things, for no one can annul (or
change) the law of nature'. The ambiguity is saying in
fact what is said by the ambiguity in the address to love in
the Proem to the third book—'whoso stryveth with yow
hath the werse'.

I cannot believe that what Chaucer understood by the
'lawe of kynde' was only that which 'dominates the fleshly
or "horsy" aspect of man', though no doubt he was aware
that this comes into the picture. He must have known
indeed that in bringing the 'lawe of kynde' into it he was
raising the problem that lies at the very core of his theme
—a problem that Alain de Lille had dealt with in the
De Planctu Naturae, and Jean de Meun in the *Roman de la*

---

[1] The only Chaucerian parallel I can find of 'ensample' followed by a
statement of what not to do contains an explicit negative: 'Beth war by this
ensample oold and playn | That no men telle hir conseil til hir wyves', *Monk's
Tale*, 2091–2.

Rose, and that Chaucer himself had made the subject of his *Parlement of Foules*.[1] And for Chaucer, as for the earlier poets, what the 'lawe of kynde' meant was almost certainly determined by medieval philosophy. 'Kynde' is a being's essential nature, which puts it in its proper species in the hierarchy of being, and since it is God himself who determines these natures and the laws of their develop/ ment, everything is subject to his laws, and therefore to the laws of its own *kynde*. It is God's love, working through nature within these beings, that causes them to achieve the perfection of (conformity to) their kinds, and to perpetuate them: that is why the attributes of Nature, in medieval philosophy, are necessity and fecundity. But what dis/ tinguishes mankind from the beast kinds, that are lower next to it in the hierarchy of being, is the possession of reason, which is the image of God in man, and with it the power of choice. Unlike the rest of creation, therefore, man can reject the government of Divine Love, and this is why, since the Fall, sexual appetite, that for beasts is natural and good, in order that they may perpetuate their species, has become necessary for him also, and is im/ planted in him by nature for the same ends. But it is not natural and good for man in the same unqualified way as it is for beasts, since it would not have become necessary for man if he had not lost the perfection of conformity to his own 'kynde', originally created in God's image, by the impairment of his reason and will. But it is a perfection he is capable of recovering, with the help of God's grace, through the natural inclination of the love divinely

[1] See J. A. W Bennett, *The Parlement of Foules: An Interpretation* (Oxford, Clarendon Press, 1957), pp. 194-212, *et passim*; and D. S. Brewer, *The Parlement of Foulys*, Nelson's Medieval and Renaissance Library (London and Edinburgh, 1960), pp. 26-30.

implanted in him, if his reason and will direct that love in the way proper to his 'kynde'. For, 'Alle thynges seken ayen to hire propre cours, and alle thynges rejoysen hem of hir retornynge ayen to hir nature' (*Consolation*, III, metrum 2). It is in this sense that 'may no man fordo the lawe of kynde', for though he may pervert the impulse of love divinely implanted in him he cannot destroy it, and that is why he cannot find true happiness outside its law. But the paradox is that while *caritas* is thus the 'lawe of kynde' for man, sexual desire, implanted in him by nature (and hence also a 'lawe' of his kind) may override the control of his reason, which is what distinguishes his kind from that of the beasts.

I think it is this paradox that Chaucer is putting to us in this whole passage. The opening line—'O blynde world, O blynde entencioun'—besides referring to Troilus' scorn of lovers refers, I think, to the 'entencioun' Philo-sophia was speaking of when she said that 'alle folk, good and eke badde, enforcen hem withoute difference of entencioun to comen to good'. She says this in Book IV, prosa 2, and the point she is making there and in prosa 3 is illustrated in the following metrum by the story of Circe, who changed men into beasts. It is the same point that Chaucer makes here, more enigmatically: the 'entencioun' is blind when we allow sexual desire to prevail over reason, for although sexual desire is natural, it is our nature to conform to a higher 'lawe of kynde' than that which we share with the beasts.[1] Yet this alternative meaning of the

---

[1] Chaucer makes the same point, I think, in the *Parlement of Foules*, when the sparrow-hawk, in reply to the goose's, 'But she wol love hym, lat hym love another', exclaims: 'Lo, here a parfit resoun of a goose!' It *is* the right way for a goose to argue, since continence in a goose would be contrary to the law of its kind. But for a human to argue like that would be to argue just like a goose—in the way the sparrow-hawk means it, and in another sense, too, since for a

ironic ambiguity does not destroy the ostensible meaning: both are a part of the whole meaning. Just as the horse that 'gynneth for to skippe | Out of the wey, so pryketh hym his corn', has to be controlled and directed by the whip, so sexual desire has to be controlled and directed by reason; but sexual desire itself is a natural and powerful force, and those 'wise, proude, and worthi folkes alle' who are addressed in the passage would do well not to scorn it, as Troilus had scorned it before he was struck by its arrows. One of the few changes that Chaucer makes in the subject-matter of the story he took from Boccaccio is to transform his hero from a man experienced in love affairs to one who mocks at love. This has sometimes been seen as evidence that Troilus is a 'purer' lover. But the change may well have been primarily to enable the poet to make this point, that sexual desire is also a natural 'lawe', and its power is not to be despised; for this, after all, constitutes the problem of sexual love—as the following stanzas of the narrator's intervention are designed to reveal:

> Men reden nat that folk han gretter wit   (I. 241)
> Than they that han be most with love ynome;
> And strengest folk ben therwith overcome,
> The worthiest and grettest of degree;
> This was, and is, and yit men shal it see.
>
> And trewelich it sit wel to be so:
> For alderwisest han therwith ben plesed;
> And they that han ben aldermost in wo
> With love han ben conforted moost and esed;[1]
> And ofte it hath the cruel herte apesed,

human to despise constancy in love, and hence continence if necessary, is to put himself on the level of a goose.

[1] Root puts a comma after 'love', which changes the meaning, and is less natural rhythmically.

And worthi folk maad worthier of name,
And causeth moost to dreden vice and shame.

Since the virtuous effect of love is stressed so strongly in the part of the narrative that follows, it is important to notice what Chaucer has done here. The first stanza derives from the description of the well where Cupid sets his snares in the garden of Deduit in the *Roman de la Rose*:

> Ful many a worthy man hath it   (1609)
> Yblent, for folk of grettist wit
> Ben soone caught heere and awayted.

And in one way what the Chaucer passage is saying is what the *Roman* says—that rank and wisdom are no pro-tection against sexual desire. But by eliminating the words 'yblent', 'caught', and 'awayted', Chaucer has removed any indication of what kind of sexual love is meant, that which blinds and enslaves or the other kind. When he goes on to describe the virtuous effect of love, it is open to the reader to judge which kind it is that has this virtuous effect, or has it more permanently. The passage concludes:

> Now sith it may nat goodly ben withstonde,   (253)
> And is a thing so vertuous in kynde,
> Refuseth nat to love for to be bonde;
> Syn as hym selven list he may yow bynde.
> The yerde is bet that bowen wole and wynde
> Than that that brest; and therfor I yow rede
> To folwen love that yow so wel kan lede.

All that is necessary to show the ambiguity of this sum-marizing stanza is to put capital letters to 'love' and 'he' and 'hym'.

This passage is perhaps the best example of how Chaucer

uses ambiguity in those of the narrator's comments that discuss the nature of love, and it illustrates one of the devices (besides the play on the word 'love') that makes the ambiguity work—namely an enigmatic and ironic use of literary allusion. Chaucer often steals from earlier writings, as he stole here from the *Consolation of Philosophy* and the *Roman de la Rose*, concepts, images, analogies, or arguments and uses them ironically by putting them, sometimes with a slight rewording, into a more ambiguous context. For example, in the *Parlement of Foules*, when the tercelet replies to the duck's scorn at the attitude of the three courtly eagles, he uses an analogy from the *Consolation*:

> Thow farst by love as oules don by lyght: (599)
> The day hem blent, ful wel they se by nyght.
> Thy kynde is of so low a wrechednesse
> That what love is, thow canst nat seen ne gesse.

In the *Consolation* this analogy is applied to those 'wrecches' whose eyes are 'so wont to the derknesse of erthly thinges that they ne may nat lyften hem up to the light of cler sothfastnesse' (IV, prosa 4). These are the ones who have allowed their 'entencioun to comen to good' to be misdirected to a false good. Are we to assume that Chaucer is ignoring the original application of the analogy, or that he gave it this different kind of reference with ironic intent ? Much has been made of the dualism of ideal and practical love in the *Parlement*, but the whole point of the unresolved squabble of the birds may be that the advocates of neither type understand the true nature of love—and it is not a part of their 'kynde' as birds that they should; but as allegory of the human kind their squabble takes on an ironic force when the courtly birds rebuke the practical birds with misapplied analogies that reveal their own ignorance of the true nature of love. There is a similar speciousness in Pandarus' analogy of the ass and the harp (1. 731-5), since traditionally the figure applies to spiritual tone-deafness, as it does in the *Consolation*.[1]

The next extended comment by the narrator comes in the Proem to the second book, before the account of Pandarus' strategy to bring Troilus and Criseyde together, and it is designed to prepare the reader for what is about to be related. The irony of its opening appeal to the Muse of history (Cleo), in a proem to that part of the story to which Chaucer contributed most of his own, is obvious enough. But what keeps it from being mere comic audacity is that, as in most of Chaucer's ironies, there is a sense in which it is true when he says 'Me nedeth here noon othere art to use'. His art will be the art of expressing through his *historia* his own viewpoint in relation to it; he will make no fundamental changes in the *historia* itself. The excuse to lovers which follows—'That of no sente'ment I this endite, | But out of Latyn in my tonge it write' —perpetuates the fiction of 'myn auctour, called Lollius', and at the same time serves to lead into what is, I think, a good example of *prosecutio cum proverbiis* as Chaucer uses that trope so frequently in this poem, to give a specious plausibility to an argument by the use of sayings in common use, held to express truths generally accepted and hence of value as 'proof' of the argument.[2] It begins:

[1] Cf. also the *Knight's Tale* (1163-71); cited by Robertson, *Preface*, p. 106.

[2] Payne observes, of Pandarus' use of proverbs: '. . . proverbs achieve currency by generalizing insight to a degree dangerously near to indiscriminate applicability, and the truth of their utterance depends after all on what is understood by the user', *The Key of Remembrance*, pp. 226-7. For Payne's own comments on the ambiguities of this Proem, which he is discussing from a some'what different angle, see p. 78.

Ek though I speeke of love unfelyngly,   (II. 19)
No wonder is, for it no thyng of newe is;
A blynd man kan nat juggen wel in hewis.

This 'self-deprecatory irony' reiterates the humility expressed in the opening stanzas of the poem where the poet
had similarly pleaded his 'unliklynesse' as a love poet.
Ostensibly the 'unfelyngly' and 'blynd' refer to the inexperience of one who has never himself 'ben at the feste'
of love, and must depend on his 'auctour'. But if we bear
in mind the way in which the poem exploits the ambivalence of the word 'love', there is an ambiguity in the
humility that the words express. The Proem continues:

Ye knowe ek, that in forme of speche is chaunge
Withinne a thousand yeer, and wordes tho
That hadden pris, now wonder nyce and straunge
Us thinketh hem, and yit thei spake hem so,
And spedde as wel in love as men now do;
Ek for to wynnen love in sondry ages,
In sondry londes, sondry ben usages.

And forthi, if it happe in any wyse,
That here be any lovere in this place
That herkneth, as the story wol devise,
How Troilus com to his lady grace,
And thenketh, 'so nolde I nat love purchace',
Or wondreth on his speche, or his doynge,
I noot, but it is me no wonderynge.

For every wight which that to Rome went,
Halt nat o path, nor alwey o manere;
Ek in som lond were al the game shent,
If that men ferde in love as men don here,
As thus, in opyn doyng, or in chere,
In visityng, in forme, or seyde hire sawes;
Forthi men seyn, ech contree hath his lawes.

The first part of the argument here follows naturally from the earlier excuse that he is only translating from his Latin 'auctour', but it is also a way of leading up to the hypothetical objection from any lover in the audience who might think, as he hears how Troilus came to win his lady's 'grace'—'that is not how I would want to win love'. This could be either an aesthetic or a moral objection, but we have been led up to it from the aesthetic angle, first by the reminder that language changes in a thousand years, so that words that had value then seem silly and strange now (which is surely something of a red herring when we have just been told that the story is a translation), and then, by an easy transition, through 'yit thei spake hem so, | And spedde as wel in love as men now do', to the proverb 'for to wynnen love in sondry ages, | In sondry londes, sondry ben usages'. This has brought us to the imaginary objection from the audience, which is countered by another (possibly ambiguous) proverb, 'Not everyone who goes to Rome keeps to the same path'.[1] But from this the argument continues, that in some lands 'al the game' would be 'shent', if they behaved openly and frankly in love 'as men don here'.[2] So what we have really been led to, by this devious route, is the 'game' that Pandarus will play, with the connivance of Troilus, in the

[1] It seems typical of Chaucer's irony to give to a familiar proverb this twist, which really perverts its meaning; cf *Astrolabe*, Prol. 39–40: 'Right as diverse pathes leden diverse folk the righte way to Rome'.

[2] The 'opyn doyng' is only one of the differences specified, but the others are so remarkably vague that it is the one that stands out: 'chere' tells us nothing unless we assume that 'opyn' applies to it as well; 'visityng', though vague, had in medieval usage, as now, a connotation of formal or official visiting; 'forme' usually implies customary or prescribed procedure; and 'seyde hire sawes', like 'chere', means little unless we take it to mean 'said what they had to say'— 'came out with it'. All the terms therefore imply kinds of behaviour that are absent in the love story that is to follow—of necessity, because of its illicit nature.

part of the story that is to follow. Has that anything to do with changing language or customs ? If 'opyn doyng' would ruin the game it is only because the game itself is an illicit one; and the proverb that 'clinches' the argument— 'ech contree hath his lawes'—has no relevance to games like that: they are played in all countries and all ages, as the narrator's innocent (but the poet's blandly ironic) 'as men don here', crediting the whole audience—or perhaps the whole country—with 'opyn doyng' in love, is calcu⁄ lated to suggest. So what had begun as an aesthetic defence of the part of the story that is to follow has taken us with unobtrusive cunning into the moral field: arguments apparently designed to help the audience to a tolerant view have become an ironic admission of its dubious character. The passage is, as it were, a demonstration in action of the narrator's limited view of his story, to which he had confessed in the earlier stanzas of the Proem. For when he pleads that he speaks of love 'unfelyngly', the 'felyng', in the medieval meanings of the word, may refer to personal understanding either emotional or intellectual. And when Chaucer habitually took up the pose of inexperience in love, he was no doubt aware that there is a close connec⁄ tion between the two. The blindness of the man who 'kan nat juggen wel in hewis' (the narrator) is intellectual as well as emotional colour⁄blindness: he cannot distinguish between the different colours that love can take, between its aesthetic and its moral aspects, between sexual passion and charitable love. Robert Payne observes that the poem 'engages us in a continuing dialectic with the narrator which defines and locates both poet and audience'.[1] The location of the poet here depends on the irony of the Proem's 'plea for tolerance' of the story that is to follow. The

[1] *The Key of Remembrance*, p. 231.

location of the audience, however, must depend on their part in the dialectic. If they accept at its face value the narrator's dialectic they will share his 'blyndnesse' and be slow, as he was, to exercise moral judgement. If they perceive the speciousness of his dialectic they will be aware, from an early stage, of his 'up´so´doun' function as a vehicle for the *sentence*, the understanding of love, both intellectually and emotionally, which is what the poem is about. But their understanding will also depend in part on their own experience as individuals. And this, I think, is what Chaucer is saying in the last stanza of his Proem:

> Ek scarsly ben ther in this place thre,   (43)
> That have in love seid lik, and don in al;
> For to thi purpos this may liken the,
> And the right nought, yit al is seid, or shal;
> Ek som men grave in tree, som in ston wal,
> As it bitit; but syn I have bigonne,
> Myn auctour shal I folwen, if I konne.

There had been an earlier reference to his 'auctour' in the introduction of Troilus' first song:

> And of his song nat only the sentence,   (I. 393)
> As writ myn auctour called Lollius,
> But pleinly, save oure tonges difference,
> I dar wel seyn, in al, that Troilus
> Seyde in his song, loo, every word right thus
> As I shal seyn . . .

This, I think, is just a joke—a mockery of the narrator's attitude to his 'auctour'. Boccaccio's poem had said only, 'E quindi lieto si diede a cantare | Bene sperando', which is in effect what Chaucer had said in the preceding stanza, 'And what to arten hire to love he soughte, | And on a song anon right to bygynne'. And the song Chaucer gives

to Troilus is a paraphrase of a sonnet of Petrarch. But we
do not need to know this to see the joke: to give 'every
word right thus' of a song (presumably composed by
Troilo) of which his 'auctour' gives only the 'sentence'
is a feat indeed on the narrator's part. In the third book,
however, there is another reference to the 'sentence' of his
'auctour', of a different kind. It comes at the end of the
account of that 'blisful nyght':

> Reson wol nat that I speke of slepe,   (III. 1394)
> For it acordeth nought to my matere;—
> God woot, they took of that ful litel kepe;—
> But lest this nyght, that was to hem so deere,
> Ne sholde in veyn escape in no manere,
> It was byset in joie and besynesse
> Of al that souneth into gentilesse.
>
> But how although I kan nat tellen al,
> As kan myn auctour of his excellence,
> Yit have I seyd, and god toforn, and shal,
> In every thing the gret of his sentence;
> And if that I at loves reverence,
> Have any thing in eched for the beste,
> Doth therwithal right as youre selven leste.
>
> For myne wordes, heere and every part,
> I speke hem alle under correccioun
> Of yow that felyng han in loves art,
> And putte hem hool in youre discrecioun,
> Tencresce or maken diminucioun
> Of my langage, and that I yow biseche . . .

The plea here is that, unlike his 'auctour', he cannot tell
'al' of the lovers' joy (and 'besynesse' is a hint of what he
means by 'al'). And, in this reference, the submission of
his words to the 'correccioun | Of yow that felyng han in

loves art' is another 'self-deprecatory irony', the 'felyng' in
love's art being that which comes from sexual experience.
But the wording gives the plea a wider reference to the
narrative as a whole, in 'have I seyd . . . and shal', and
'myne wordes, heere and every part', and in this wider
reference the 'felyng in loves art' may also take a wider and
deeper meaning. We are reminded of the famous aphorism
which Chaucer applies to love in the opening stanza of
the *Parlement of Foules*, 'The lyf so short, the craft so long
to lerne', where the 'craft' (*ars*) applies to love in a wider
context than the lovers' bed. Or the 'art' may mean, in a
closely related medieval sense of the word, what we
would now call the 'science', or philosophy of love.[1] To
refer to 'felyng in loves art' in these meanings is appropriate
in the context of medieval thought, where love was a
primary subject of philosophy, and where 'moral problems
. . . were essentially problems of love'.[2] It is these wider
and deeper meanings that help to give the plea to the
reader to 'correct' the poet's words its ambiguity; he is to
read into them ('Tencresce'), or take them with a pinch
of salt ('maken diminucioun') at his own discretion,
which will depend on his own 'felyng in loves art'.[3] The
'sentence' of his 'auctour' which the poet claims to be
preserving could be either the substance or gist, as it is in
the Lollius passage, or it could be the 'meaning' or
significance. What the poet has 'in eched for the beste'
therefore could be additions which he thought necessary

[1] See *OED*, s.v. Art, sense 3 b.

[2] See D. W. Robertson, *Preface*, p. 462, *et passim*.

[3] Payne writes of this passage: 'The submission of the poem to the "correction,
increasing, and diminution" of those who have "feeling" for its subject matter
may be an attempt to indicate the part the reader's response is to play in the
total efficacy of the poem', *The Key of Remembrance*, p. 76. It is the ambiguity
of the words 'felyng' and 'art' that I have tried to define more fully.

to make clearer the gist-of his author's story, or amplifica‑
tions which, in his opinion, give the 'beste' meaning to the
story. The whole passage thus has a comic ambiguity:
what appears to be a modest plea that although he cannot
describe all the lovers' joy he has tried his best to give the
gist of his author's account, is an ironic admission that he
has amplified it 'at loves reverence', and that it is for the
reader to respond according to his own understanding of
love, emotional or intellectual.

This passage has been discussed out of its turn because
of its similarity to the Proem to Book II. The next major
intervention by the narrator in that book follows the scene
where Criseyde, after hearing from Pandarus of Troilus'
love for her, sees the hero himself riding past her window
as he comes straight from battle:

> Criseyda gan al his chere aspien,　　　　　　　　(II. 649)
> And leet it so softe in hire herte synke,
> That to hire self she seyde: 'who yaf me drynke?'

And she blushed at her own thought, remembering that
this was the man her uncle swore would die unless she
had pity on him; and, 'for pure ashamed', she quickly
pulled in her head from the window:

> And gan to caste and rollen up and down　　　(659)
> Withinne hire thought his excellent prowesse,
> And his estat, and also his renown,
> His wit, his shap, and ek his gentilesse;
> But moost hire favour was, for his distresse
> Was al for hire, and thought it was a routhe
> To sleen swich oon, if that he mente trouthe.

The narrator, however, is not content to leave it at that,
and adds:

Now myghte som envious jangle thus: (666)
'This was a sodeyn love; how myghte it be
That she so lightly loved Troilus
Right for the firste syghte, ye parde?'
Now whoso seith so, mot he nevere ythe;
For every thyng, a gynnyng hath it nede
Or al be wrought, withouten any drede.

For I sey nat that she so sodeynly
Yaf hym hire love, but that she gan enclyne
To like hym first, and I have told yow whi;
And after that, his manhod and his pyne
Made love withinne hire for to myne;
For which, by proces and by good servyse,
He gat hire love, and in no sodeyn wyse.

Yet Criseyde's exclamation, 'who yaf me drynke?', is an
echo of Lavinia's words in the French romance *Eneas*,
where the love was so sudden that she felt she had been
given a love potion. Charles Muscatine, who draws
attention to the parallel and to the 'pointed contradiction
between narrative and dramatic action' here, comments
that the narrator's 'sympathy and his occasional ignorance
contribute to the ambiguity of Criseyde'.[1] But the ambiguity may lie in the way the narrator's comment is worded.
When he tells us that it was 'by proces and by good
servyse' that Troilus 'gat hire love, and in no sodeyn
wyse', this is true if 'gat hire love' refers, euphemistically,
to her final yielding. But in raising the question 'how
myghte it be | That she so lightly loved Troilus | Right for
the firste syghte?', is the poet not calling attention to what
his narrator is ostensibly refuting, and giving it validity by
the irony of his refutation? There is something suspicious
about a refutation that begins so lamely—'For every thyng,

[1] *Chaucer and the French Tradition*, p. 154.

a gynnyng hath it nede'—and that does not, after all, produce any good reasons to convince us that she did not love lightly. For even if we overlook the ambiguity of his denial of the suddenness of her love, we may still feel that the case he puts up is an ambivalent one: if Troilus' 'manhod' and 'pyne' are enough (after her first inclining to 'lyke' him) to make 'love withinne hire for to myne', is it surprising that Diomede's 'manhod' and 'pyne' can do the same? What may make it seem surprising is that, unlike Boccaccio's Griseida, whose readiness to become Troilo's mistress prepares us for her readiness to become Diomede's, Criseyde proves difficult to bring to the point of yielding to Troilus (hence the validity of the narrator's defence of her, in that meaning of his words). The difference is usually seen as a radical change of her character by Chaucer; but this is something that must depend on what we mean by 'character'. When Chaucer chose to translate his story into the more courtly terms of French romance, it was necessary to change the behaviour, or deportment, of his heroine. And, as Karl Young put it, Criseyde 'is purged of Griseida's hearty sensuality, which is alien to the manners of romance, and assumes a tender circum spection characteristic of romantic heroines such as Ydoine, Fénice, Lydaine, and the Dame de Fayel'.[1] But Chaucer must have been well aware that his heroine's part in the action does not lend itself to the courtly role, and seen the potentialities for irony that the incongruity would afford. For where in French courtly romance does the lady main tain the 'forme of daunger' so persistently, only to betray for another the lover she has been brought with such difficulty to accept? It is true that Chaucer's picture of his

---

[1] 'Chaucer's *Troilus and Criseyde* as Romance', *PLMA* liii, N.S. xlvi (1938), p. 44.

heroine is altogether less harsh and crude than Boccaccio's, but the difference may lie primarily in the very different purposes of the two poets, which is at its most obvious in their roles as narrators. It was not to Chaucer's purpose to discredit his heroine as a person or as a woman: his interest in her character is primarily as it relates to the love problem itself. When he intrudes, as narrator, in the passage under discussion, it is to 'elicit an attitude' from the reader to the part of the story he has just related, to raise indeed the question that he does raise—whether Criseyde loved too lightly—and to anticipate the ironical enigma of her long resistance to Troilus. The reader who takes at its face value what he says, in spite of its ambiguity and ambivalence, will of course see her character as radically different from that of Griseida, and moreover find an incongruity between her resistance to Troilus and the comparative ease with which she transfers her love to Diomede. But there is incongruity only if we allow the narrator to confuse us by persuading us to accept as evidence that she did not love lightly what is really evidence only that she knew how to behave with 'tender circumspection'. There is nothing to belie the picture of her courtliness, and the picture is an attractive one: she has all the beauty, wit, delicacy of feeling, and tenderness controlled by perfect decorum, that characterize the courtly heroine. But, as the narrative makes clear at the beginning, there is in her the tendency to love easily that is the cause of her fickleness as it was in her prototype. Since it is Criseyde's love that is to prove unstable, it is fitting that the question whether to love at first sight is to love too lightly should be raised at this point. Troilus, too, loved at first sight, but, as we have seen, when the narrator intervened in a similar way to comment, it was to raise a different question about the nature of the love. In Troilus'

love sexual desire overruled the control of reason and so
developed into an idolatrous passion: Criseyde's love is fed
by worldly, and largely self-regarding considerations, and
so it is these considerations that influence her in her change
of heart. In her reflections after her exclamation 'who yaf
me drynke ?', she had listed Troilus' 'gentilesse' (after his
'shap') as one of the favourable factors, but when we are
told, immediately after the narrator's intervention, that
'Troilus persone | She knewe by syghte, and ek his genti-
lesse', we have another unobtrusive hint of just what that
'gentilesse' can have meant to her at this stage.[1]

The narrator's interventions in the third book, though
more numerous than in the first two, do not, I think, raise
important new questions for the reader, but serve to stress
or develop questions already raised. This is the book that
brings us to the consummation of the love, and that is the
focal point to which the interventions are directed. They
often take the form of sexual innuendo—as when the
narrator remarks, after telling how Troilus awaited the
fulfilment of Pandarus' promise to bring the lovers
together at his house:

> I nyl nat seyn that, though he lay ful softe,   (III. 442)
> That in his thought he nas somwhat disesed;
> And that he torned on his pilwes ofte,
> And wolde of that he missed han ben sesed,—
> But in swich cas men ben nought alwey plesed,
> For aught I woot, no more than was he—
> This kan I deme of possibilitee.

Or later, when the lovers are in bed: 'Reson wol nat that
I speke of slepe . . .' (1394).
Sometimes, however, the ambiguity in the narrator's

[1] See Alan T. Gaylord, '*Gentilesse* in Chaucer's *Troilus*', p. 26.

interventions in this book is at the narrator's expense—as
when he exclaims, when Troilus is at last in Criseyde's
arms:

> O sooth is seyd, that heled for to be   (1212)
> As of a fevere or other gret siknesse,
> Men moste drynke, as men may alday se,
> Ful bittre drynke; and for to han gladnesse,
> Men drynken ofte peyne and gret distresse;
> I mene it here as for this aventure,
> That thorugh a peyne hath founden al his cure.

For the reader may be aware, as the narrator seems determined not to be, that the 'cure' that Troilus has found is
only a palliative for the fever he is suffering from (as he
remarks to Pandarus later in the same book 'I hadde it
nevere half so hote as now'), and that the bitter drink of the
pain and distress he has already suffered is nothing to the
bitterness he will have to drink later.

But probably the subtlest of the ironies at the narrator's
expense comes at the end of the book, in the account of the
virtuous effect of love on Troilus, where (as in the portrait of the Prioress) the irony is not overtly critical—there
is only a gentle emphasis on irrelevancies ('And moost of
love and vertu was his *speche*', and 'glad was he if any
wyght wel ferde | That lovere was'), and some ambiguity:

> For soth to seyn, he lost held every wyght   (1793)
> But if he were in loves heigh servise,
> I mene folk that oughte it ben of right.
> And over al this, so wel koude he devyse
> Of sentement, and in so unkouth wise
> Al his array, that every lovere thoughte
> That al was wel what so he seyde or wroughte.

It would be difficult to imagine a more equivocal com-
mendation of the effect of love on Troilus.

In the Proem to the fourth book what irony there is serves as an unobtrusive transition from the double role the poet had adopted in relation to his story to his more direct attitude of the last two books:

> For how Criseyde Troilus forsook,   (IV. 15)
> Or at the leeste how that she was unkynde,[1]
> Moot hennesforth ben matere of my book,
> As writen folk thorugh which it is in mynde.
> Allas! that they sholde evere cause fynde
> To speke hire harm! and if they on hire lye,
> Iwis, hem self sholde han the vilanye.

There is still a note of ironic *naïveté*, but whereas earlier the shifting of responsibility to his 'olde bokes' had increased rather than lessened the sting of the irony, here the rather touching reluctance of the narrator to 'speke harm' of his heroine helps to prompt our sympathy in advance. There is little direct intervention in the narrative of this book, and when it is ironic the irony is not at the narrator's expense. For example, after Criseyde's long declamation to Troilus of her grief at the thought of leaving him and her vows to be true to him (twenty-three stanzas), the narrator comments:

> And treweliche, as writen wel I fynde,   (IV. 1415)
> That al this thyng was seyd of good entente;
> And that hire herte trewe was and kynde
> Towardes hym, and spak right as she mente . . .

Here narrator and poet are one: there is no ambiguity, and if there is irony it is at the expense of Criseyde.

In the fifth book there is no Proem, and the first comment by the narrator (50–6) is to explain why Troilus did not

[1] For a discussion of the meaning of *unkynde*, see Appendix, pp. 145 ff.

kill Diomede, as he thought of doing—he was afraid that Criseyde would die if she heard of it, 'lo, this was al his care'. The next two (267–73 and 722–5) are to evoke the reader's feeling for the suffering, first of Troilus, then of Criseyde ('Thow, redere, maist thi self ful wel devyne | That swich a wo my wit kan nat defyne', and 'In al this world ther nys so cruel herte . . . That nolde han wepen for hire peynes smerte'). And in a similar vein is the often-quoted passage which comes after Criseyde's defection and her self-denunciation ('allas! for now is clene ago | My name of trouthe in love for evere mo'):

> Ne me ne list this sely womman chyde,   (1093)
> Forther than the storye wol devyse.
> Hire name, allas, is punysshed so wide,
> That for hire gilt it oughte ynough suffise.
> And if I myghte excuse hire any wise,
> For she so sory was for hire untrouthe,
> Iwis, I wolde excuse hire yit for routhe.

The *naïveté* of the narrator has gone completely: this is the voice of the mature, humane poet himself. There is no need for irony at this stage, since what the irony was designed to reveal about the nature of Criseyde's love is now self-evident.

In the next of the narrator's comments, though there may be a double meaning, it is not an ironic one:

> But, natheles, men seyn that at the laste,   (1639)
> For any thyng, men shal the sothe se.

This refers to Troilus' realization at last of Criseyde's betrayal; but the reader, too, is nearing the end, when the whole truth must be seen. And although there is another glimpse of the ironic Chaucer, in his plea to 'every lady bright of hewe' not to blame him for Criseyde's guilt

(1772-85), it is more in the nature of a *jeu d'esprit* than anything else—when he claims that in saying that he would
rather tell of the faithfulness of Penelope or the good
Alceste, he is thinking not only of 'thise men', but mostly
of women who are betrayed. This is reasonable enough,
but only an ironist would use such reasoning to conclude
a story of woman's fickleness with the warning, 'beth war
of men'.

The last of the narrator's interventions, which follows on
from this, is perhaps the most interesting of them all:

> Go, litel book, go, litel myn tragedye,   (1786)
> Ther god thi makere yit, or that he dye,
> So sende myght to make in som comedye!
> But, litel book, no makyng thow nenvie,
> But subgit be to alle poesie;
> And kis the steppes, where as thow seest space[1]
> Virgile, Ovide, Omer, Lucan, and Stace.

Here the poet is speaking as poet, not as narrator: though
it is an intervention in the narrative it does not refer to any
part of it, but to the poem as a poem. And we can see, once
again, Chaucer's agility in turning what he has found in
his literary sources to his own poetic ends. Boccaccio had
also addressed 'piccolo mio libretto' in a long envoy at the
end of his poem, and he too had mentioned Virgil, Ovid,
Lucan, and Statius, but in a very different way from
Chaucer: Boccaccio's 'little book' is to leave Virgil to the
great writers, Ovid is only for successful lovers, Lucan and
Statius for soldiers. Chaucer's injunction to his 'litel book'
to kiss the steps of these writers echoes Statius' own warning
to his book, the *Thebais*, not to emulate the *Aeneid*—'nec tu

---

[1] 'Space' in the sense 'walk' (see *OED*, s.v. Space, vb. 6) Some manuscripts have 'pace', which many editors prefer, but the manuscript authority
favours 'space' (see Root's note).

divinam Aeneida tempta, | Sed longe sequere, et vestigia semper adora'. The five poets listed by Chaucer are the five great narrative poets of antiquity, and for his poem to kiss their footsteps is a gesture of humility in face of their greatness. But there is something more than humility expressed in the passage. This is one of the many passages in Chaucer's poetry where he refers to his art, or task, as a poet;[1] and it is important to understand the distinction he is making here between comedy and tragedy, and the meaning of his somewhat enigmatic pun on 'makere', 'make', 'makyng'. The pun is possible because 'make' was formerly used in various applications where verbs of more specific meaning would be used now; so that 'making' could mean the making of a book, or even more specifically, poetical composition, while still retaining its primary meaning. Thus when the poet prays God to grant that the maker of this little tragedy may 'make' in some comedy before he dies, and tells his little book not to envy any 'makyng' but be subject to all poetry, in one relevance he is giving 'makyng' its more basic sense, and implying a distinction between 'makyng' and subjection to poetic tradition. For 'alle poesie' implies the tradition of poetry, and poetic tradition to the medievals would be, as Robert Payne observes:

. . . what was nearest to stability in human knowledge: the preserved record of what is constantly meaningful to all men in all times and places, and therefore a record of the way in which temporal events reflect eternal purposes.[2]

It is in this relevance perhaps that Chaucer is making a distinction between comedy and tragedy, for tragedy more

[1] See Robert Payne, *The Key of Remembrance*, for a perceptive analysis of these passages; for a reference to this passage, p. 84.

[2] p. 46.

than comedy, is the vehicle for tradition of this kind. If God grants the maker of this little tragedy to 'make in some comedie', it must not envy any 'makyng' but 'subgit be to alle poesie', content to be a small link in the great chain of poetic tradition.

Payne's analysis of this stanza in the light of Chaucer's evident consciousness of poetic tradition has done much to explain the impression it makes on the reader—an impression of poetic meaning far deeper than that conveyed in the similar envoys of Boccaccio or Statius. And it makes more meaningful also the relevance of the following stanza. For corruption of the text through 'miswriting' due to the 'grete diversite' of dialect and spelling, of which the poet is conscious, could be, and of course was, a contributory factor not only in the 'mismetring' of his poem, but also to some extent in distorting or concealing its sense. And when he adds, 'And red wherso thow be, or elles songe, | That thow be understonde, god I biseche', he may have been thinking not only of the possible effects of such miswriting, but of the enigmatic nature of his own expression. The major revisions he made in the poem were all to underline its moralistic meaning, and the narrator's interventions for the greater part of the poem had been to remind the audience or reader of the part they must play in the understanding of the poem. Here, as he sends his 'litel book' out into the world affectionately, as a father might send his son, it is God, not the audience, he beseeches, for it is for the understanding of posterity that he is praying.

It could be objected that to find ironic ambiguities or specious dialectic, as I have done, in the narrator's interventions is to be too clever. If we look for it we can find speciousness where it is clearly not intended—for example, in the fourth book of Wordsworth's *Prelude*, where he uses the image of a child putting a shell to his ear and hearing its 'mysterious union with its native sea', to express by analogy the ear of faith which hears 'Authentic tidings of invisible things, | Of ebb and flow, and everlasting power'; for what the child hears of course is not the authentic voice of the sea, but noises in its own head. But here we have a very different poetic mind from Chaucer's, and a very different poem from *Troilus and Criseyde*. In Chaucer's poetry, as it develops, there are increasing signs of his mastery of oblique and devious methods of expression, and there was everything in his literary environment to encourage it. As D. W. Robertson writes of the stylistic figures, many of which were used in the passages that have been quoted in this chapter: 'Medieval students un- doubtedly learned about them in school, observed their appearance in both sacred and profane texts, and acquired a taste for using them in their own writings.'[1] And Chaucer had good training for using them in the French poets who were his favourite reading. It was probably from them especially, for example from Jean de Meun, that he learned how to use specious dialectic to ironic effect. And F. Whitehead has demonstrated a good example of 'reason leading to *desraison*' in the arguments by which the go-between in Chrétien's *Yvain* manages to persuade Laudine to accept the idea of a match with her husband's slayer.[2] And in spite of the different nature of the two poems, there is a similar inference to be drawn:

. . . the God of Love, to make a true lover happy, can adopt very devious tactics and can show himself shameless, cynical,

[1] *Preface*, p. 288.
[2] 'Yvain's Wooing', *Medieval Miscellany, Presented to Eugène Vinaver* (Man- chester Univ. Press, 1965), pp. 321–36.

and unmindful of any but his votaries. From time to time in the narrative, the author very unobtrusively allows the real character of the God and his worshippers to show through.[1]

In Chaucer's poem the speciousness and ambiguities of the narrator's interventions, in the first three books especially, call attention to the 'showing through' in the narrative itself.

[1] 'Yvain's Wooing', pp. 333–4.

CHAPTER IV

Ambiguity and the Narrative

To separate what the narrator of *Troilus and Criseyde* says in his own person from what he says in his narrative may be convenient, but in a study of the ambiguity of the poem the distinction can be somewhat unreal. For example, the songs and lyrical invocations put into the mouths of the persons in the story serve in much the same way as do the narrator's interventions to draw attention to the focal point of the part of the story in which they occur, and with similar ironic ambiguity. And we find the same use of specious dialectic in the speeches of Pandarus, Troilus, and Criseyde as we find in the narrator's comments. Even the description of the reactions of the characters to each important turn of events has an ironic ambivalence, which is sometimes underlined in the narrator's comment; for these reactions are often depicted in imagery that is itself ambivalent. The figures are usually those familiar in both medieval love poetry and doctrinal exposition (many of them occur frequently in the *Consolation*), and this double application enables them to be woven into the fabric of the ironic presentation of the story. But the irony does not depend on the reader's consciousness of the doctrinal application of these images: it is the way the images are used, dynamically, in varying forms, in different types of context, with shifts of relevance, that gives them their ironic force. There are unobtrusive changes of tone, ambiguities or paradoxes which qualify the significance of the images in

various ways, making them into a kind of running com⁄
mentary within the narrative itself.

In the early part of the story the most frequently repeated
figures are those that relate to love's 'tender trap', its duress
its 'malady' or 'fever', and the 'fire' that is the cause of
the fever. After Troilus saw Criseyde in the temple, 'love
bigan his fetheres so to lyme' that he could only with
difficulty hide from his companions the change that had
come over him. And in the days that followed, love

> held hym as his thral, lowe in destresse,   (1. 439)
> And brende hym so in sondry wise ay newe,
> That sexti tyme a day he loste his hewe.

And he is often driven to reflect:

> O fool, now artow in the snare,   (1. 507)
> That whilom japedest at loves peyne;
> Now artow hent, now gnaw thin owen cheyne . . .

Love robs him of his sleep and makes 'his mete his foo',
and the 'siknesse' shows in his colour at all times so that
he has to pretend he has a fever, lest it should be guessed
that the hot fire of love is burning him (1. 484–90). The
cause of his 'siknesse' he confesses to Pandarus is the
'desir' which burningly assails him (1. 607), and when
he had sought to assuage the burning with the sight of
Criseyde, 'ay the ner he was, the more he brende', for, as
the narrator observes to the audience, 'ay the ner the fir, the
hotter is,— | This, trowe I, knoweth al this compaignye'
(1. 449–50). And though he tried to hide his love, as
Pandarus tells Criseyde, 'wel the hotter ben the gledes
rede, | That men hem wrien with asshen pale and dede'
(11. 538–9).

These images are given a further significance in Troilus'
first song, when he asks:

... if that at myn owen lust I brenne,   (1. 407)
From whennes cometh my waillynge and my pleynte?
If harme agree me, wherto pleyne I thenne?

For, though he does not know it, he answers his own
question in another image:

> ... thus possed to and fro,   (415)
> Al steereles withinne a boot am I,
> Amydde the see, bitwixen wyndes two,
> That in contrarie stonden evere mo.[1]

Thus when Pandarus contrives his plan for a meeting with
Criseyde at Deiphebus' house, and instructs Troilus to
feign sickness, Troilus' reply—

> iwis, thow nedeles   (II. 1527)
> Conseilest me, that siklich I me feyne;
> For I am sik in ernest, douteles,—

has a dramatic ambiguity, directed to the audience.

When Pandarus had come into the picture we had the
image of the 'leche' added to that of the 'siknesse', and at
first it is Pandarus himself who is to be the 'leche'. Even
before Troilus has divulged the name of the lady, Pan-
darus tells him, 'who so list have helyng of his leche, | To
hym byhoveth first unwre his wownde' (1. 857-8), and
after he has confessed to Pandarus and been promised help,
he is

> lik a man that hurt is soore,   (1. 1087)
> And is som deel of akyng of his wownde
> Ylissed wel, but heeled no deel moore,
> And, as an esy pacyent, the loore
> Abit of hym that gooth aboute his cure.

---

[1] D. W. Robertson points out that this image derives (through Petrarch)
from Proverbs 23: 33-4: 'Thy eyes shall behold strange women, and thy heart
shall utter perverse things. And thou shalt be as one sleeping in the midst of the
sea, and as a pilot fast asleep when the stern [i.e. rudder] is lost' (*Preface*, p. 478).

But just before the first meeting between Troilus and Criseyde, when all the company, with Criseyde present, is discussing Troilus' 'siknesse', and 'every wight gan wexen for accesse | A leche anon' and suggests cures, 'ther sat oon, al liste hire nat to teche, | That thoughte: "best koude I yit ben his leche"' (II. 1581–2).

This, image, too, is qualified, however, when the narrator intervenes to comment, when Troilus at last is lying in Criseyde's arms:

> O sooth is seyd, that heled for to be   (III. 1212)
> As of a fevere or other gret siknesse,
> Men moste drynke, as men may alday se,
> Ful bittre drynke; and for to han gladnesse,
> Men drynken ofte peyne and gret distresse;
> I mene it here as for this aventure,
> That thorugh a peyne hath founden al his cure.

For the last two lines, instead of insuring that the reader applies what he has said to 'this aventure', have the opposite effect—they suggest (almost as though the narrator himself has become uneasily aware of the possibility) that the analogy could apply to Troilus in a different way. Similarly another significance is given to the 'fire' image later, when Pandarus is trying to rouse Troilus from the despair into which he has fallen at the thought of losing Criseyde:

> Swich fir by proces moot of kynde colde.   (IV. 418)
> For syn it is but casuel plesaunce,
> Som cas shal putte it out of remembraunce.

As the narrator comments,

> Thise wordes seyde he for the nones alle,   (428)
> To helpe his frende, lest he for sorwe deyde;
> For douteles to don his wo to falle
> He roughte nat what unthrift that he seyde.

But though it may be true that Pandarus' words are 'un-thrift' in the sense that they are said only to try to alleviate Troilus' suffering, there is dramatic irony in the fact that what is said as a comfort for Troilus would be no comfort if he applied it to Criseyde. On the face of it, the issue at this point seems to be between the 'practical' viewpoint and the courtly ideal of constancy in love, as it seems to be also in the bird debate of the *Parlement of Foules*. And on the face of it, it is the latter we are invited to admire. But the real issue, or problem, that Pandarus' words must raise is what constitutes 'trouthe' in love. For what he says is true in terms of the philosophy of love the poem is expounding: such 'fire', as Troilus' 'fire' has been described to us, by its very nature must cool in the process of time, and since the joy it offers is a gift of fortune ('casuel plesaunce') and not true happiness, a turn of Fortune's wheel ('Som cas') can put it out of mind. This is what happens with Criseyde's fire, in her love for Troilus. Pandarus' words serve to remind us that, for all his suffering, the fire of Troilus' love has a physical origin, is love for a gift of fortune.

Closely interwoven with the imagery of the fire of love, and the fever or sickness it causes, are images of light and darkness in various forms. When Pandarus says, as he takes away the candle on that 'blisful nyght', 'Light is nat good for sike folkes yen', there is more to his words than their sexual innuendo, if we see them in relation to the whole pattern of imagery in this first love episode (for example, Troilus' 'For I am sik in ernest, douteles'). And here perhaps the most relevant passage is the one in which Antigone's song had occurred. This also provides a useful example of the function of the songs in relation to the narrative. They serve as commentary, usually veiled, on what has just been related, and one way in which they do this is by taking up images that had been used in the narrative and giving them a new ambiguity. Antigone's song may have been suggested to Chaucer by the *Paradis d'Amour* of Guilluame de Machaut, in which a lady expresses her gratitude to love and praises it as the source of all virtues and the enemy of vice.[1] But the wording is his own, and he uses the song to provide one of a series of fortuitous factors that combine to overcome Criseyde's reluctance to consider a love affair with Troilus, for it 'happens' to answer, point by point, the fears she had been dwelling on in her reflections before she joined Antigone in the garden.[2] In those reflections, Criseyde had first persuaded herself that it would do her no shame to 'set her heart at rest' upon this knyght, if she kept her 'honour' and her 'name':

> But right as whan the sonne shyneth brighte, (II. 764)
> In March, that chaungeth ofte tyme his face,
> And that a cloude is put with wynd to flighte,
> Which oversprat the sonne as for a space,
> A cloudy thought gan thorugh hire soule pace,
> That overspradde hire brighte thoughtes alle,
> So that for feere almost she gan to falle.
>
> That thought was this: 'allas! syn I am free,
> Sholde I now love, and putte in jupartie
> My sikernesse, and thrallen libertee? . . .
>
> For love is yit the moste stormy lyf,
> Right of hym self, that evere was bigonne;
> For evere som mystrust, or nice strif,
> Ther is in love; som cloude is over that sonne . . .'

[1] See G. L. Kittredge, *MLN* xxv (1910), p. 158.

[2] See Sister Mary Charlotte Borthwick, 'Antigone's Song as "Mirour" in Chaucer's *Troilus and Criseyde*', *MLQ* xxii (1961), pp. 232–5.

The analogy in the first stanza here is curious: the cloudy thought overspreading Criseyde's bright thoughts ought to equate with the cloud overspreading the sun in March, but in fact it is the other way round. I think the clue to the paradoxical expression in this stanza comes shortly after, wards in Antigone's song, in those stanzas that appear to provide a reassuring answer to this part of Criseyde's reflections. They are a defence of love against its detractors; for after affirming 'This is the righte lif that I am inne, | To flemen alle manere vice and synne', the lady of the song goes on to say:

> And whoso seith that for to love is vice,   (855)
> Or thraldom, though he feele in it destresse,
> He outher is envyous, or right nyce,
> Or is unmyghty, for his shrewednesse,
> To loven; for swich manere folk, I gesse,
> Defamen love, as nothing of it knowe;
> Thei speken, but thei benten nevere his bowe.
>
> What is the sonne wers, of kynde right,
> Though that a man, for feblesse of his eyen,
> May nat endure on it to see for bright?
> Or love the wers, though wrecches on it crien?
> No wele is worth, that may no sorwe dryen.
> And, forthi, who that hath an hed of verre,
> Fro caste of stones war hym in the werre!

These stanzas of the song seem to provide a refutation of Criseyde's fears that love will 'thrallen libertee' and that 'som cloude is over that sonne'. The first stanza seems to be saying that those who say that love is vice or thraldom are those who have never been struck by love's arrows. R. K. Root comments in his note to these lines: 'Hazlitt records the proverb: "Many talk of Robin Hood that

never shot in his bow". Chaucer transfers the bow to
Cupid.' But does he? Is there not a kind of pun on the
proverb that leaves open the question what kind of love
experience is meant? In the second stanza the analogy of the
man with eyes too weak to look on the sun has a similar
ambiguity: it is applied to those who defame love, but it
applies also, by implication, to those they are defaming
('Why blame the sun itself if there are some with eyes too
weak to look on it?'). Those who defame love itself because
there are some whose eyes are too weak to look on the
radiance of the 'sun' of love are as bad as those they
defame, like people in glass houses throwing stones; for
they do not know the true nature of love either: 'Thei
speken, but thei benten nevere his bowe'.

Thus the song does not say that the kind of love Criseyde has in mind is not thraldom, or that there is no
'cloude over that sonne': what it says, in effect, is that the
cloud is really the feeble sight of those who cannot look
upon love's 'sun'. Antigone's song is thus the counterpart,
in relation to Criseyde, of the narrator's comment, 'O
blynde world, O blynde entencioun . . .', in relation to
Troilus; and there is a similar oblique allusion to ideas
expressed in the *Consolation*. The whole complex of the
imagery of sun/cloud/feeble sight is used there many times,
where the 'wrecches' are those who 'have their eien so
wont to the derknesse of erthly thynges that thei ne may
nat lyften hem up to the light of cler sothfastnesse'. It is
only by the 'light of his ynwarde sighte', if he will use it,
that man can see what the 'blake cloude of errour' covers,
namely that what love is really seeking is the 'soverayne
good', which is the 'sun' of love. This, I think, explains
the paradoxical application of the sun/cloud analogy
to Criseyde's reflections before she entered the garden.

Momentarily 'a cloude is put with wynd to flighte' when
a 'cloudy thought' passes through her 'soule', overspread,
ing all her 'brighte thoughtes'; for this 'cloudy thought' is
really a glimpse of the truth. But it is only a passing glimpse,
for she fails to see the ambiguity of Antigone's song.

What this part of the narrative tells us about Criseyde
is that her hesitation about entering into a love affair with
Troilus is a real hesitation at this stage—not the coyness of
a Griseida only waiting to be persuaded—but it is founded
on worldly, and self regarding considerations. For she has
no understanding of love. The lady of the song had said
that she was 'trewe' in her 'entente', and after the song is
ended, Criseyde asks: 'Who made this songe now with so
good entente?'. And when she goes on to ask, somewhat
wistfully: 'lord, is ther swych blisse amonge | This loveres
as they konne faire endite?', Antigone answers:

> Ye, wis, . . .   (887)
> For al the folk that han or ben on lyve
> Ne konne wel the blisse of love discryve.
>
> But wene ye that every wrecche woot
> The parfit blisse of love? why nay, iwys!
> They wenen al be love, if oon be hoot;
> Do wey, do wey, they woot no thyng of this!
> Men mosten axe at seyntes if it is
> Aught faire in hevene; why? for they kan telle;
> And axen fendes is it foul in helle.

But 'Criseyde unto that purpos naught answerde'. Antigone's words of course, like her song, leave open the
question which 'hevene' is meant, but the relevance to the
problem of love that is troubling Criseyde is clear enough.
Like all who love, Criseyde has the 'entencioun to comen
to good': when she asked who made the song 'with so
good entente', it was because it seemed to hold out to her

a picture of the 'parfit blisse' which she, like all who love, is seeking. But her eyes are 'too wont to the derknesse of erthly thynges' to be able to look up to the 'sun' of true bliss, and so the distinction Antigone makes between the 'parfit blisse of love' and the heat of sexual passion is lost upon her.

Thus in the same way that Chaucer's alteration of the character of Troilus, from that of an experienced lover to one who had always scorned love, had a close relevance to the moralistic, or philosophical, theme, so too has the change in the character of Criseyde, which makes her hesitate to embark on a love affair. In terms of character her hesitation springs from her 'ferfulnesse', but this 'ferful-nesse' becomes a way of giving her part in the story its philosophical relevance. Where Troilus had succumbed at once to the god of love, although he had just been observ-ing in lovers the very things that give Criseyde pause— the 'dredful joie' of lovers and the 'stormy lyf' of love—it is Criseyde, ironically, who is deterred from yielding to her first inclination to love by the fact, among other things, that 'men ben so untrewe'. And where Troilus, in his first song, is concerned with the bewildering effects of love, it is Criseyde who is troubled by considerations of its nature, and its ultimate end:

> To what fyn is swich love, I kan nat see,   (II. 794)
> Or wher bycometh it, whan it is ago . . .
> That erst was no thing, into nought it torneth.

Thus her 'ferfulnesse', which as a trait of her character is one of the factors that helps to enlist our sympathy for her, becomes a way of using her to raise philosophical questions about love. The irony of it is that Criseyde herself, whose love turned into nothing, is the one to see that this is the nature of this kind of love: her question 'To what fyn is swich love?' is one that is central to the poem's morality. What Root calls her 'fatal weakness—the inability to make a deliberate choice'[1] is motivated more deeply by a concern for her happiness, and a suspicion of the kind of happiness that a love affair can hold out for her. It is fitting therefore that in the bedroom scene, when Pandarus comes to tell her that Troilus has just arrived in great distress because he has heard that she loves another, she sees in this a confirmation of her fears, which she expresses in her speech on false felicity. Dramatically, her speech is not very happy: philosophy sits awkwardly in the mouth of a lady, newly roused from sleep, confronted with such a situation, and more so in the mouth of a Criseyde who, we know, already had her suspicions that some such situation was intended. Her speech is in keeping with her character, however, and has a dramatic ambiguity directed mainly to the audience. For Criseyde can see that worldly joy is unstable, just as she could question 'to what fyn' is the kind of love she was contemplating—for these are matters that can be understood on the worldly level. What she cannot see is the connection between the two, for this demands spiritual understanding.

The ambiguity of Criseyde lies less in her character as such than in Chaucer's method of using his persons for an evaluative purpose. But to say this is not to deny the subtlety of his characterization in the more modern meaning. To recognize how cleverly he solves the technical problem of expressing his morality through his story, we must recognize also his genius for selecting the revealing gesture, speech, or thought, which, in this poem, characterize his people with a realism that goes far beyond mere allegorical

[1] *Troilus and Criseyde*, p. xxxii.

type. He excels in letting his persons give themselves away, and in this poem the process reveals a psychological insight beyond anything that had been revealed before in English literature. For example, in the scene just referred to, he records Criseyde's reactions thus:

> This accident so pitous was to here,   (III. 918)
> And ek so lik a sooth at prime face,
> And Troilus hire knyght to hir so deere,
> His prive comyng, and the siker place,
> That though that she dede hym as thanne a grace,
> Considered alle thynges as they stoode,
> No wonder is, syn she dide al for goode.

What is revealed here is of course relevant moralistically: the hint, in 'so lik a sooth at prime face', that Criseyde may not have been entirely convinced by the 'accident' that 'so pitous was to here', and the inclusion of the 'prive comyng' and the 'siker place' among the considerations that moved her to admit Troilus, must qualify the meaning of 'goode' in the last line. But the account also gives a life-like impression of the tension between what her feelings would like her to believe and what her shrewdness suspects, between what her love is urging and a caution that must satisfy itself that it will be safe. It is 'psychological' enough to recognize that behaviour may be determined by very mixed and confusing motives, and, stylistically, in its inconsequence and near-incoherence, it is a remarkable depiction of a state of mind.

It is not until the fourth book, however, when the separation of the lovers is imminent, that there begins to come into the depiction of Criseyde that touch of exaggeration—comic distortion of a characteristic or attitude—that there is at times in the depiction of all three of the main characters, which is the most conspicuous evaluative component of 'character' (as it is in graphic caricature). Two examples come to mind, of quite distinct kinds—one in her lament when she hears the news that she is to be exchanged for Antenor, and the other in her last speech to Troilus. In her lament she cries:

> To what fyn sholde I lyve and sorwen thus? (IV. 764)
> How sholde a fissh withouten water dure?
> What is Criseyde worth from Troilus? . . .

And she resolves to starve herself to death ('syn neither swerd ne darte | Dar I noon handle, for the crueltee'), and to wear black as token, in Troilus' absence, of the 'obser-vaunce' of her 'ordre', which will be 'sorwe, compleynte, and abstinence'. And she bequeaths to Troilus her heart and 'the woful goost therinne' to complain eternally with his spirit:

> For though in erthe ytwynned be we tweyne,   (788)
> Yit in the feld of pite, out of peyne,
> That hight Elisos, shal we be yfeere,
> As Orpheus with Erudice his fere.

Griseida's 'vestimento nero' had been to testify to her 'widowhood': the change to a nun's habit gives a sharper point to the dramatic irony ('abstinence'); and thus the irony which depicts her intention to be true to Troilus in this extravagant rhetoric becomes a way of bringing her later failure more pointedly into the present picture, so that we are aware, at one and the same time, both of the fervency of the intention and of the failure—which must qualify, even at this point, the value of the intention, give it a kind of hollowness, even though she means it in all good faith. And the ineptitude of her choice of Orpheus and Eurydice as an analogy for the eternal reunion of her spirit with Troilus' becomes still more pointed in view of the moralistic meanings that were attached to the Orpheus legend from the sixth century onwards. Her lament is a counterpart to Troilus' several laments which precede it, and his, too, contain a classical analogy:

> My dethe may wel out of my brest departe   (IV. 470)
> The lif, so longe may this sorwe myne;
> But fro my soule shal Criseydes darte
> Out nevere mo; but down with Proserpyne,
> Whan I am dede, I wol go wone in pyne;
> And ther I wol eternaly compleyne
> My wo, and how that twynned be we tweyne.

It is almost symbolic of the difference between their two characters, especially as seen in their different attitudes to their pending separation, that Troilus can see only eternal parting and 'pyne', while Criseyde envisages a reunion of their spirits in a comparatively comfortable 'Elisos' ('oute of peyne'). And it is typical of Chaucer's sensitive hand, ling of his story that Criseyde's protestations here of her intention to be true to Troilus have less pathos than her later, more simple, 'To Diomede algate I wol be trewe'.

In Criseyde's last speech to Troilus, at the end of the fourth book, the irony is more subtle, less dependent on dubious rhetoric. At the close of her speech she tells Troilus why she loved him:

> For trusteth wel, that youre estat roial,   (IV. 1667)
> Ne veyn delit, nor only worthinesse
> Of yow in werre or torney marcial,
> Ne pompe, array, nobleye, or ek richesse,
> Ne made me to rewe on youre destresse;
> But moral vertu, grounded upon trouthe,
> That was the cause I first hadde on yow routhe.

This is adapted from part of the speech that Boccaccio had

given to Troilo in praise of Griseida, and one critic comments:

> Chaucer, a greater and more humane poet . . ., by transferring the valediction to Criseyde, allowed the great betrayer a final moment of integrity and dignity. Thus he gave full value to the faithfulness of intention before going on to record in the next book the faithlessness of the action ensuing.[1]

But while it is true that it was cruder to give the speech to Troilo in praise of 'the great betrayer', does the trans⁄ference not, in fact, make Criseyde the victim of the irony in another way? In Boccaccio's version it was Troilo who was deceived in Griseida: the different, and more subtle, irony which gives the speech to Criseyde reveals her capacity for self⁄deception. For whether we take 'rewe on youre destresse' and 'first hadde on yow routhe' to refer to her first inclination to look with favour on Troilus, or as euphemisms for her eventual yielding, it is difficult to see where his 'moral vertu' had come into the picture. It is true that there had been a mention of moral virtue in connection with Troilus, when Pandarus in his first talk with Criseyde had seized upon the opening that her inquiry about Hector gave him to mention

> ek his fresshe brother, Troilus, (II. 157)
> The wise, worthi Ector the secounde,
> In whom that alle vertu list habounde.

And Criseyde had replied:

> . . . treweliche I holde it grete deynte, (164)
> A kynges sone in armes wel to do,
> And ben of good condiciouns therto;

[1] A. C. Spearing, *Criticism and Medieval Poetry* (Edward Arnold, London, 1964), p. 115.

For grete power and moral vertu here
Is selde yseyn in o persone yfere.

But the nearest she gets to moral virtue in the factors she
lists among the considerations that move her, after her
first sight of Troilus, to think 'it was a routhe | To sleen
swich oon, if that he mente trouthe', is his 'gentilesse',
which she puts after his 'shap'. And in this final speech
to Troilus we have another of the several hints of what
'gentilesse' means to her.[1] For she goes on to say:

> Ek gentil herte and manhod that ye hadde,   (IV. 1674)
> And that ye hadde, as me thoughte, in despit
> Every thyng that souned into badde,
> As rudenesse and poeplissh appetit,
> And that youre resoun bridlede youre delit,—
> This made, aboven every creature,
> That I was youre, and shal, whil I may dure.

It is in this stanza, I think, that we have the clue to the
main reason why Chaucer gave this speech to Criseyde,
but that is a point that must be deferred to a discussion of
its relevance to Troilus. What it reveals in Criseyde is her
priorities: she may think she loves Troilus for his moral
virtue, but what she admires most is his gentlemanly
behaviour.

The view that Chaucer radically changed the character
of his Criseyde usually goes hand in hand with the view
that there is a radical difference in her responses to the two
lovers. But it is significant, I think, that as far as the direct
descriptions of Criseyde are concerned, what we have in
the first part of the poem refers to her appearance and
social demeanour, and it is only when Diomede is about

---

[1] See Alan T. Gaylord, 'Gentilesse in Chaucer's *Troilus*', pp. 25–7, for a
full illustration and discussion of this point.

to approach her, in the scene which immediately precedes her decision to remain in the Greek camp, that we are given a description of her character, in any moral connotation of the word:

> And with hire riche beaute evere more   (v. 818)
> Strof love in hire ay, which of hem was more.

> She sobre was, ek symple, and wys withal,
> The best ynorisshed ek that myghte be,
> And goodly of hire speche in general,
> Charitable, estatlich, lusty, and fre;
> Ne nevere mo ne lakkede hire pite;
> Tendre herted, slydynge of corage.

In the medieval meanings of the words these are the qualities in Criseyde that have been illustrated in the foregoing narrative, though the 'slydynge corage' has only been hinted at. The amorousness that was so obvious in Griseida is less obvious in Criseyde, since it is controlled by her decorum, but we had a glimpse of it at the very outset, in her exclamation at her first sight of Troilus, and it is clear from various hints later. For her reaction to Pandarus' unmistakable declaration of his intention at their first meeting, after he has overcome her initial shock ('Whan ye ben his al hool, as he is youre; | Ther myghty god yit graunte us see that houre', to which she replies, 'Nay, therof spak I nought, a ha! . . . ye shenden every deel') is indication enough that she knew from the first exactly what was wanted to her, and so her 'innocence' at her first meeting with Troilus—

> I wolde hym preye   (III. 124)
> To telle me the fyn of his entente;
> Yit wiste I nevere wel what that he mente.—

is a part of the comedy, a gentle mockery of the courtly

nature of Troilus' protestations, and her eventual answer is a mimicry of his own ambiguous courtly language. But Pandarus' jubilation at that answer, and his promise to arrange another meeting at his house, though they indicate what he understands her to mean, call forth no protest from her. Together with the ready pity and the tender heart, it is the amorousness that determines her response to both lovers—without it there would have been no occasion for her 'tender circumspection'. And in this aspect there is no radical alteration of her character.

It is Criseyde's circumspection that makes necessary the expansion of the whole of the first love episode. With-out it, there would have been no need for the machinations of Pandarus, which Chaucer adds to the story. In the earliest version, in the *Roman de Troie* of Benoit de Sainte Maure, the story had comprised the second love episode only, in which Briseida, sent from Troy to the Greek camp, forgets her love for Troilus and becomes the mistress of Diomede. In Boccaccio's version, which supplies a first part to the story to tell how Griseida became Troilo's mistress, the betrayal is still the thing. In Chaucer's poem there is a shift of emphasis so great that we might almost say that the second love episode has become subsidiary to the first, a necessary appendage to it. For whereas the 'hearty sensuality' of Griseida's response to Troilo is enough to explain her similar response to Diomede, Criseyde's 'tender circumspection' makes the link between the two love episodes less obvious; but it is there all the same, in the way the second love episode follows the pattern of the first—in the words of John Speirs, it sounds like 'an inferior and degraded replica' of it.[1] The point that Chaucer is making—the point that required the expansion

[1] *Chaucer the Maker* (Faber & Faber, London, 1951), p. 79.

of the first love episode—can be illustrated best by an analysis of the similarities between the two episodes, in this case as they affect Criseyde.

When Diomede speaks of love to her for the first time, as he conducts her from Troy to the Greek camp, Criseyde 'unto that purpos lite answerde', for she was so oppressed with sorrow that she hardly heard what he said (v. 176–9); but when he speaks to her of love later, she gives him the same sort of equivocal answer she gave to Pandarus/ Troilus—if she were to 'han routhe' on any Greek it would be Diomede, and 'I sey nat therfore that I wol yow love,| Ny sey nat nay' (1000–4).[1] But when she went to bed that night:

> The brighte Venus folwede and ay taughte   (v. 1016)
> The wey, ther brode Phebus down alighte;
> And Cynthea her charhors overraughte
> To whirle out of the Leoun, if she myghte;
> And Signifer his candeles sheweth brighte.

This is to tell us that the ten days are nearly over, before the end of which she had promised Troilus she would return to Troy; but the paradox of the evening star both following and teaching the way to the setting sun alerts us to some more poetic, symbolic meaning, suggests the star of love both following the setting of Troilus' sun in her heart and helping it to set. For just as in the earlier love episode it was after her exclamation 'who yaf me drynke?' that she had begun to reflect on the advantages of having

[1] It is interesting to note that Chaucer is not following Boccaccio here. He follows Benoit in making Diomede speak of love to Criseyde already at their first meeting—this suits his picture of the 'sodeyn' Diomede; but he transposes to the later scene her equivocal reply (taken from Benoit and, probably, Guido delle Colonne's epitome of Benoit as well). To have left it as it was in his source would have detracted from his picture of Criseyde's grief at leaving Troilus, and given a vulgarity to her behaviour that he did not want.

Troilus as her lover, so now it is after Venus has 'taughte
the wey' that she begins to waver in her resolution to keep
her promise to return to Troy:

> Retornyng in hire soule ay up and down   (1023)
> The wordes of this sodeyn Diomede,
> His grete estat, and peril of the town,
> And that she was allone and hadde nede
> Of frendes help. And thus bygan to brede
> The cause whi, the sothe for to telle,
> That she took fully purpos for to dwelle.

As Robert Payne observes: '. . . the love's star following the
sunset before pale moonrise in effect expresses Criseyde's
decision before she has consciously made it'[1]—hence the
symbolic force of 'Signifer his candeles sheweth brighte'.
It is the crucial decision she is about to make, and she
rationalizes it as she had rationalized the first prompt-
ings of her love for Troilus, and as the ladies of French
courtly romance often rationalize their love. The rest
follows with all too foreseeable inevitability.

Again, however, it is the lover's 'pyne' that is the occasion for her final yielding:

> And for to hele hym of his sorwes smerte   (1049)
> Men seyn, I not, that she yaf hym hire herte.

The narrator's 'I not' here is like his earlier denial that she
loved Troilus too lightly—a half-hearted echo, and even
less calculated to convince; for who, if not the story-teller,
should know? Its perfunctoriness is typical of the tone of
the narration in this second love episode; for while this
episode follows the pattern of the first, it does so with a
conspicuous haste and a lack of the feeling of active involvement that characterized the earlier account. The difference

---

[1] *Key of Remembrance*, p. 201.

is appropriate, since what the fuller treatment of the earlier episode had been designed to reveal obliquely of Criseyde's character, or attitude to love, is now self-evident: the change of tone only stresses what the similarity of pattern demonstrates. Where Troilus' 'estat' had been one of several features to influence her, Diomede's is the only one to be mentioned, for the 'tender circumspection' that had informed her attitude when she was her 'owene womman, wel at ese' among friends in Troy is forced to become somewhat cruder now. And it is not so easy for her to maintain the 'forme of daunger' with the 'sodeyn Diomede' as it was with the 'gentil' Troilus and the uncle Pandarus who understood the situation so well. She goes through the motions, but with a difference that has its own pathos, as well as its irony.

As a person, Criseyde steals the picture from Troilus, partly because of the teasing enigma her behaviour seems to present, and partly because she is depicted more realistically, especially in her scenes with Pandarus. But for the theme of the poem in its totality it is Troilus who is the more important figure; and one of the gains of recent criticism has been to reinstate him as the focus of the poem's meaning. Charles Muscatine writes: 'The fact is, that as medieval romance goes, as the "code" goes, Troilus is *too* perfect a courtly lover'.[1] And he sees this exaggeration of Troilus' courtliness as complementary to the exaggeration of the role of Pandarus as go-between. For while Pandarus is the literary descendant of a long line of go-betweens in French romance and *fabliau*, he does far more going-between, far more persuading and advising, than any of his ancestors. Perhaps the supreme example of the

[1] *Chaucer and the French Tradition*, p. 137.

complementary nature of the roles of Troilus and Pandarus, in Chaucer's expansion of them, is when Pandarus
thrusts the fainting Troilus into Criseyde's bed and tears
off his clothes to the 'bare sherte' (III. 1097–9). Quoting
this passage, Muscatine observes: 'This is the first time in
medieval literature that the go-between must go so far as
actually to pick up the hero and throw him into the
lady's bed.'[1]

In Muscatine's view of the poem, Troilus exemplifies
both the 'very real virtues' of courtly idealism and also
its weaknesses; while Pandarus illustrates 'the wholesome
sanity of ordinary life', as well as 'the shadow of futility
cast over any human activity' in which the more spiritual
values are neglected.[2] But if that is one side of the picture
that the two complementary roles present with relevance
to the morality, there is another which puts the 'courtly
idealism' of Troilus in a more dubious light. This side
shows itself most obviously in the scene where Pandarus,
after having successfully contrived the first meeting between
Troilus and Criseyde, chooses this moment to take stock
of the situation. He reminds Troilus that ever since he
saw him suffering for love he has 'don his bisynesse' to
bring him to joy, and has now brought him to stand 'in
weye to faren wel'. But he adds:

> I seye it for no boost;   (III. 248)
> And wostow whi? for shame it is to seye:
> For the have I bigonne a gamen pleye
> Which that I nevere don shal eft for other,
> Although he were a thousand fold my brother.
>
> That is to seye, for the am I bicomen,
> Bitwixen game and ernest, swich a meene

---

[1] *Chaucer and the French Tradition*, p. 152.   [2] Ibid., p. 131.

As maken wommen unto men to comen;
Thow woost thi selven what I wolde meene; . . .

I think this must be the first time a go-between has an-
nounced so plainly what he (or she) is doing. Pandarus'
excuse is that he did not do it for 'coveitise', 'But oonly
for tabregge that distresse, | For which wel neigh thow
deidest, as me thoughte.' In his reply Troilus is even more
explicit:

> me thoughte, by thi speche, (395)
> That this which thow me doost for compaignie,
> I sholde wene it were a bauderye.
> I am nat wood, al if I lewed be;
> It is nat so, that woot I wel, parde.
>
> But he that gooth, for gold or for richesse,
> On swich message, calle hym what the list;
> And this that thow doost, calle it gentilesse,
> Compassioun, and felawship, and trist;
> Departe it so; for wyde wher is wist,
> How that ther is diversite requered
> Bytwixen thynges like, as I have lered.

And to prove the distinction between what is 'bauderye'
and what is only like it, he offers to procure for Pandarus
his fair sister Polixene, Cassandra, Helen or 'any of the
frape'; however fair she may be or 'wel yshape', Pandarus
has only to name her and leave it to him (407–13).

This is strange 'proof' indeed, but as Alan Gaylord
remarks, 'The *gentilesse* that is affirmed by such rationaliza-
tion becomes a semantic barrier preventing acknowledg-
ment of the true state of things'.[1] And it is a barrier that
operates not only within the story but between the story
and the modern reader; for, strange as it may seem, this

[1] '*Gentilesse* in Chaucer's *Troilus*', p. 29.

passage does not seem to have troubled those critics who
see Troilus as a pure and noble lover. It is passed over,
perhaps as mere hyperbole, largely because the aura of
'gentilesse' created by the courtly language acts as a veil
between the reader and the narrative: we tend to see the
persons of the story in the light of their own values, their
own premisses, and their own methods of reasoning, as if
they belonged to a different world. And it is this view that
'Chaucer himself' seems to be encouraging in his 'plea for
tolerance' in the Proem to the second book. But it is
passages such as the one just cited that must make us
suspect irony in his plea. For what Troilus is claiming to
prove, in his repudiation of Pandarus' suggestion of
'bauderye', is the validity of Pandarus' own excuse that
what is done 'for compaignie' is different from what is done
'for coveitise', but he goes further than Pandarus when he
tries to prove that it is different in *kind*, by referring his
proof to the distinction between 'thynges like', which is
the logical distinction between likeness and identity of
substance. But what Pandarus is doing *is* 'bauderye', in the
only meaning of the word that could be relevant: he *is*
acting as procurer for Troilus, whatever may be his
reasons for doing it. And Troilus' generous offer to do the
like for Pandarus only underlines the fallacy of his 'proof'.
It is in ways like this that the poem 'engages us in a continuing dialectic with the narrator', and not only with the
narrator speaking for himself, with his narration of the
story too. It does so, without seeming to do so, by raising
questions of moral judgement and refuting them with
arguments that may seem valid on first impression, but
which are really arguments that give the case away.
What we learn from such a passage or scene is an ironic
pointer to Troilus' attitude: he is only too willing to fall

in with Pandarus' way of looking at things. Significantly, his speech on this occasion is by far the longest he has spoken yet, and there is an unwonted animation in his anxiety to still Pandarus' doubts, when he adds, after his offer to do the like for Pandarus:

> But sith thow hast idon me this servyse,   (414)
> My lif to save, and for non hope of mede,
> So, for the love of god, this grete emprise
> Parforme it out; for now is most nede.

It is hints such as this that must qualify the surface impression that Troilus is a passive figure only. And they must lend an irony to his attitude in the fourth book, when he hears that Criseyde is to be exchanged for Antenor—not only to his long speech proving that 'al that comth, comth by necessitee', but also to his 'curteisye' in taking no steps to prevent Criseyde's departure. The focal point of this book is the separation of the lovers; and when Troilus first hears, in the Trojan 'parlement', of the proposed exchange, he 'wel neigh deyde', and he has only two thoughts—to save her 'honour' and to prevent her going:

> Love hym made al prest to don hire bide, (IV. 162)
> Or rather dyen than she sholde go;
> But resoun seyde hym on that other syde:
> 'Withoute assent of hire ne do nat so,
> If thow debate it, lest she be thy fo,
> And seyn, that thorugh thy medlynge is iblowe
> Youre bother love, ther it was erst unknowe'.

This stanza derives from *Il Filostrato*, and is the only one of several references in this book to the reason/desire conflict which has its counterpart there. Siegfried Wenzel, who was the first to call attention to this significant fact, observes that whereas Boccaccio represents Troilo as in a state of indecision, Chaucer has his Troilus already here deciding on his course of action: 'the stanza which im-mediately follows (with no counterpart in Boccaccio) tells that Troilus "gan deliberen for the beste" (169) that he would inform his lady of the "parlement's" decision, and then follow her wishes in the matter (169–75).'[1] Wenzel notes the difference as evidence that Troilus is the more *curteis* lover. But is it an accident that in the next stanza we are told how Hector spoke up with indignation against the proposal—'Sires, she nys no prisoner . . . We usen here no wommen for to selle'?

The next reference to the conflict of reason and desire is similar, and comes in a similarly ambiguous context, in Troilus' reply to Pandarus, who has urged him:

> Why nylt thy selven helpen don redresse,   (528)
> And with thy manhod letten al this grame?
> Go ravysshe hire; ne kanstow nat, for shame?

To which Troilus answers with a series of arguments, the last of which reiterates his anxiety to save her 'honour':

> Thus am I with desir and reson twight: (572)
> Desir for to destourben hire me redeth;
> But reson nyl nat, so myn herte dredeth.

This reiteration is the occasion for the third reference to reason, by Pandarus in his reply:

> Devyne nat in resoun ay so depe,   (589)
> Ne curteisly, but help thi selve anon.

The last of the references to reason in this book comes in Criseyde's last speech, in praise of Troilus, which has already been referred to ('And that youre resoun bridlede youre delit').

---

[1] 'Chaucer's Troilus of Book IV', pp. 542–3.

It seems clear enough that these repeated references to the reason/desire conflict in this book are to stress the *curteis* application of reason by Troilus. But what are the inferences to be drawn? Wenzel, after observing that the conflict between reason and desire is a commonplace of moral thought reaching back to Plato, and also that in medieval courtly love poetry it is usual for reason to oppose the love, suggests:

Perhaps Chaucer's use of the reason-vs.-desire conflict is an expression, not so much of courtly-love conventions as of the wider courtly and chivalric ethos. Chivalry and courtesy, as an ideal of life, rested on rationality, on the subordination of personal desires to universal norms embodied in a particular social structure. Courtly love, as only one aspect of that ideal, was commonly thought to be the great social and psychological power to educate the knight in the perfect behaviour of his class. Whatever else Troilus stands for in Chaucer's poem, he is foremost the ideal representative of that courtly ethos.[1]

But this, surely, is precisely what is at issue. To reconcile his view of Troilus with the morality of the poem Wenzel writes:

I would suggest, then, that inherent in the entire *Troilus and Criseyde* is a structure of three levels of values: the realms of sensuality, of noble courtly love, and of 'divine speculation'. Troilus and Criseyde, but pre-eminently Troilus, live in a world of *courtoisie*, where reason controls low appetites, where love of a noble woman raises the lover's character to the heights of refinement, of social graces, and of moral virtues, where such love is based on service and total submission to the lady's desires. This noble realm is neatly distinguished from the world of sensuality, of low manners, of Bayard the farm horse.[2]

[1] Ibid., p. 544.   [2] Ibid., p. 546.

This 'structure of three levels of values' is reminiscent of C. S. Lewis's 'triple scale of values' by which he explained Chaucer's 'praise of love' in the earlier books of *Troilus* and his 'rejection of love' at the end of it: 'The apparent inconsistency results from the fact that medieval writers are using a triple scale of values where their modern critics are using only a double one.'[1] But Wenzel's way of putting it makes it easier perhaps to make a case against the theory. This distinction between the noble realm of *courtoisie* and 'the world of sensuality, of low manners' is exactly the distinction Criseyde herself was making in her last speech to Troilus, when she claimed that it was for his 'moral vertu' that she first had pity on him, and then went on to explain that she loved him most of all for his 'gentil herte' and 'manhod', and because he scorned ('as me thoughte') 'Every thyng that souned into badde, | As rudenesse and poeplissh appetit'. But gentility is one thing, moral virtue is another; low manners are one thing, sensuality is another. And it was not 'poeplissh appetit', as Criseyde means it, that Bayard the farm horse had signified. Just as in the *Parlement of Foules* the turtle-dove's defence of constancy in love must signify that constancy is not a monopoly of the courtly class, so the Bayard analogy must signify that sexual appetite is not exclusively 'poeplissh', for the 'worthiest and grettest of degre' can be overcome by it. Criseyde was expressing the courtly view when she commended Troilus—'that youre resoun bridlede youre delit'; for it would be irrational in a *curteis* lover to treat his lady with 'rudenesse' in love; but is such 'rudenesse' the

---

[1] Review of E. K. Chambers, *Sir Thomas Wyatt and Some Collected Essays*, *Medium Aevum*, iii (1934), p. 239. Eugène Vinaver observes, however: 'I cannot follow Mr C. S. Lewis in his attempt to attribute the triple scale of values to "medieval writers" generally. . . . There is certainly no such thing in the French *Queste*' (Introd. to *Malory*, p. lxxvii.).

only realm of sensuality? When Reason herself in the *Roman de la Rose* of Jean de Meun shocked the courtly lover by the 'rudenesse' of her outspoken description of the castration of Saturn, she defended herself: it is not wrong to name by their proper name those things which her Father created with his own hand in Paradise (6955–60). In the more courtly, and more subtle and ambiguous *Roman de la Rose* of Guillaume de Lorris, and in Chaucer's *Troilus*, there is a greater recognition of the value, and the beauty, of *courtoisie*, but it is made clear enough that it is *courtoisie* as it is applied by the servants of the god of love, not courtesy as it relates to moral virtue. There may be an area of overlapping—it is admirable in any circumstances to abstain from pride, or rudeness, or incontinence—but the motives are different. And this is why Reason opposes the god of love. It is rational to foresee the consequences of discourteous behaviour, and it is on this level of rationality that Troilus follows reason against desire in taking no action to prevent Criseyde's departure; but the Reason which in Guillaume's *Roman* tries to persuade the lover to resist the domination of the god of love is not merely this rational insight into the consequences of an action; it is a responsible moral force which gives man the power to choose how he will act, and, as the image of God in man, reason's prime function is to control and direct to its proper end the love divinely implanted in him. So, in the same way that the garden of Deduit itself is only a deceptive copy, a travesty, of a different kind of garden, as Genius tells us at the end, so too it is a travesty when Troilus, in this fourth book, attributes to the triumph of reason over desire a decision to take no action, which is really a decision dictated by the dilemma to which the conquest of desire over reason had brought him in the first place. It is true that 'he adheres to the courtly ethos, even though he thereby falls "out of joie"',[1] but he would have been free to act as Hector acted if he had listened to reason earlier. In spite of his *curteisye* it is not the 'worthi Ector the secounde' who cuts the more admirable figure.

It is ironic, therefore, that Criseyde, at once his victim and his fellow sufferer, encourages him in his 'curteisye', and when he proposes that he should steal her away, tells him that people would say that it was not love that prompted him, but 'lust voluptuous and coward drede':

> Thus were al lost, ywys, myn herte deere,   (1574)
> Youre honour, which that now shyneth so clere.

And her own 'honeste' she sees as something that 'floureth yit' but would be 'spotted with filthe', if there were scandal—'and that were routhe and synne' (1576–82). And it is in this ironic context that we have another of the references to reason in this book, when she adds: 'And forthi sle with resoun al this hete.'

If any of these five references to reason in this book had stood alone, it would be foolish to read into it the weight of ironic meaning that I have done. But the way in which Chaucer has caught up the one allusion to the reason/ desire conflict in *Il Filostrato* and stressed it by this insistent reiteration must alert suspicion. The persistence of the allusion to what is essentially a moralistic concept, and one that in medieval love poetry is commonly used in that way, serves to show up how little moralistic relevance this *curteis* application of it has. And that, I think, may have been Chaucer's main motive in transferring the speech of praise at the end of the book from Troilo to Criseyde. For it is this speech that provides the opening for the ironic

---

[1] Wenzel, 'Chaucer's Troilus of Book IV', p. 545.

contrast between 'moral vertu' and 'poeplissh appetit', and for the insertion of the idea of reason bridling 'delit', which is not in Troilo's speech, and which is a revealing ironic climax to the other references to reason.

Alan Gaylord has shown how Chaucer uses the terms 'gentil' and 'gentilesse' to veil a gradual transition from the association with 'moral vertu', in Pandarus' first mention of Troilus to Criseyde, to something more am/ biguous. And I think this may be of relevance also to the evident contrast there is in the poem between Troilus and Diomede. 'As the "code" goes', the contrast is great. Diomede does not love at first sight: when he had to con/ duct Criseyde from Troy to the Greek camp he reflected that he might as well have something for his trouble, for 'He is a fool that wol foryete hym selve', and so he speaks to her of love—without effect (v. 92–179). And later he sets about contriving,

> With al the sleighte, and al that evere he kan,   (773)
> How he may best, with shortest taryinge,
> Into his net Criseydes herte brynge.
> To this entent he koude nevere fyne;
> To fisshen hire, he leyde out hook and lyne.

These of course are the terms in which Pandarus thought of the earlier love situation: as Muscatine observes, 'Dio/ mede is Pandarus again in his power of speech and in his tactical sense, in his idiom and in his gesture'. But (more disturbingly),

Chaucer improvises for this 'sodeyn', tactical Diomede the air of a Troilus, too:

> And with that word he gan to waxen red,   (v. 925)
> And in his speche a litel wight he quok,
> And caste asyde a litle wight his hed,

And stynte a while; and afterward he wok,
And sobreliche on hire he threw his lok,
And seyde, 'I am, al be it yow no joie,
As gentil man as any wight in Troie'.[1]

It is these similarities, together with the similarity in
Criseyde's reactions, that make Diomede's wooing read
like 'an inferior and degraded replica' of the wooing by
Pandarus and Troilus. Of course the comedy in the stanza
just quoted is clear enough, but in Chaucer's comedy there
is often a sting. Which of the two lovers is being degraded
in this stanza? As a person, I think, Diomede: when
Troilus behaved like this there was none of the suggestion
of play-acting that there is here. But if we take 'gentil' in
its highest sense, is there anything to choose between them?
Diomede's claim to be 'As gentil man as any wight in
Troie' is, on this higher level of meaning, putting to us the
question whether it is any less 'gentil' to do your own
fishing with hook and line than to have someone do it for
you. The impression of degradation in the 'replica' of the
second wooing derives mainly, I think, from the way in
which it reminds us only too well that we have been
through all this before.

Pandarus' part in the ambiguity of the narrative depends
largely on the depiction of him as both an exponent of the
doctrine of courtly love and a practical realist. He was
both already in *Il Filostrato*, and, as Muscatine observes,
'Chaucer, in stretching that poem, stretched this character
on the same form'. Thus Pandarus provides 'a view of
courtly love under the aspect of realism', his 'deeper realism'
serving to test the 'greater spirituality of Chaucer's Troilus
and the more formidable difficulty of Criseyde'.[2] But what

[1] *Chaucer and the French Tradition*, p. 163.   [2] Ibid., pp. 138 and 139.

is the effect of the test? The 'idealism' of Troilus and the 'practicality' of Pandarus are certainly used to give a 'very round, very comprehensive view of the values of human experience', as Muscatine observes. But when he writes that 'Beyond this lies another level of perspective', we may question the separation that this implies. He adds:

Chaucer is a spiritual pupil of Boethius. He sees in turn the whole sphere of human experience against eternity. He sees the imperfection inherent in any mode of life—be it practical or idealistic—wherein the end itself is *earthly* joy, and hence wherein the prize may at any moment be washed away by the same tides that brought it in.

It is true that Muscatine sees these 'two levels of perspec⁄ tive' as 'intimately related', but only by implication:

To dwell at length on the attractiveness of earthly love and then to repudiate all in a palinode is neither philosophical nor artistic. But to present secular idealism as a beautiful but flawed thing, and to present practical wisdom as an admirable but incomplete thing, to present them, indeed, as antithetical and incongruous to each other, is by implication to present a third view, higher and more complete than either.[1]

But it is not; unless there is something in the mode of presentation to indicate what this higher view is. He adds: 'This philosophical third view hovers over every important sequence in the *Troilus* . . .'—but there must be something in the sequences to make it hover. And this is where the ambiguity of Pandarus comes in. For though he may be 'stretched on the same form' as Pandaro, in the sense that the dualism inherent in Pandaro (as devotee of courtly love and as practical realist) is deepened and developed,

[1] Ibid., pp. 131–2.

his dual role also makes him the vehicle for ironic ambiguities of a kind that had no place in Boccaccio's poem.
He is not given any of the major lyrical invocations or
songs which, as we have seen, act as commentary by their
ambiguity: his doctrine is always of direct practical application to the situation in hand. But nevertheless he is, as an
exponent of courtly-love doctrine under a practical aspect,
a channel for cogent comment that has ironic ambiguity.
For example, when he tells Troilus that now that he is
'converted out of wikkednesse' by the 'goodnesse' of the
god of love, he will be the best pillar of love's order:

> Ensample why: se now thise grete clerkes,   (1. 1002)
> That erren aldermost ayeyn a lawe,
> And ben converted from hire wikked werkes,
> Thorugh grace of god, that list hem to hym drawe,
> Thanne arn they folk that han moost god in awe,
> And strengest feythed ben, I undirstonde,
> And konne an errour alderbest withstonde.

In itself it is a reasonable argument, but, like the arguments
by which the go-between in *Yvain* persuades her mistress
to accept the idea of a match with her husband's slayer, it is
'reason leading to *desraison*', as it is applied to Troilus'
'conversion' to an illicit love. It is passages like this that
justify D. W. Robertson's view of Pandarus as 'a blind
leader of the blind, a priest of Satan'. But Pandarus is
clear-sighted enough on a practical level—more so than
either Troilus or Criseyde—and his clearer vision makes
him a natural channel for comment of a different kind,
that is, where the practical view serves to show up the
fallacy of the 'courtly' view. That is Pandarus' role in the
part of the poem already discussed, where Troilus refuses
to take any action to prevent Criseyde's departure. When
Pandarus urges—

> Why nylt thy selven helpen don redresse,   (IV. 528)
> And with thy manhod letten al this grame?
> Go ravysshe hire; ne kanstow nat, for shame?

his words help us to see Troilus' passivity for what it is:
Troilus *cannot* redress the 'grame' by his 'manhod', since
the situation must prevent him 'for shame' from carrying
her off. And when Pandarus replies to Troilus' explana-
tion, 'Desir for to destourben hire me redeth; | And reson
nyl nat, so myn herte dredeth', with the words

> Devyne nat in resoun ay so depe,   (589)
> Ne curteisly, but help thi selve anon . . .

he is putting his finger on the weakness of Troilus' position.
This scene provides a good illustration of Muscatine's
point, that the 'courtly' and 'practical' viewpoints offset
one another, to show up the strengths and weaknesses of
each. For while Pandarus' choice of words ('manhod',
'manly', 'help thi selve') put Troilus' failure to take
action in a less flattering light than does Troilus' own view
of it, at the same time Pandarus' practical advice to
'ravysshe' Criseyde lays him open to moral judgement,
when we remember that to excuse his treachery to Criseyde
he had trusted and implored Troilus to 'save alwey hire
name'. If the morality of the part that Pandarus plays in
the poem is that 'practical wisdom is an admirable but
incomplete thing', it is also that, to act from feeling alone,
without some bedrock of principles to guide the feeling,
is to build on shifting sand. He could act as procurer
for Troilus out of sincere feelings of friendship and pity
for him, and preach to him the courtly ideals of constancy and of protecting his lady's 'honour', but when the
crisis comes he can only suggest, out of the same feelings
of friendship and pity, 'Whi nyltow love an other lady

swete?', and when that fails, 'Go ravysshe hire'. His
practical wisdom is inadequate when it comes to the test,
not because he cannot understand the idealism of the
courtly 'code', but because the position to which his own
amoral interference has helped to bring Troilus leaves only
two choices for Troilus, to offend against the 'code', or to
suffer the loss of Criseyde. The feeling that had prompted
Pandarus to interfere, to rouse Troilus from his passivity
before he won Criseyde, prompts him now to similar
amoral advice:

> Lat nat this wrecched wo thyn herte gnawe,   (621)
> But manly set the world on sixe and sevene;
> And if thow deye a martyr, go to hevene.

But Troilus would rather suffer than offend his lady. Each
attitude may invite our sympathy for the feeling that
prompts it: neither is admirable moralistically. Pandarus'
advice advocates a complete disregard for other people, but
what he says has some truth as applied to Troilus: if
'hevene' lies in physical union with Criseyde, the 'martyr-
dom' which Troilus fears need not be a deterrent.

In the fifth book the inadequacy of Pandarus' practical
wisdom becomes more overt, while at the same time it
serves to underline the obsessional nature of Troilus' love:

> Troilus,   (v. 323)
> My deere frende, as I have told the yore,
> That it is folye for to sorwen thus,
> And causeles, for which I kan no more.
> But whoso wol nat trowen red ne loore,
> I kan nat sen in hym no remedie;
> But lat hym worthen with his fantasie.

We cannot doubt the sympathy he feels for Troilus, and
must feel pity for his helplessness; but we can also see the

blindness which prevents him from realizing—even now—
that it was from following his 'red' and 'loore' that Troilus
is in this situation. His practical wisdom is enough to
enable him to see the 'fantasie' of Troilus' belief that
Criseyde will return, but it is not enough to make him see
the futility, and the cruelty, of encouraging him in his
fantasy. Only when Troilus himself is forced to see the
truth, does Pandarus give up his misguided efforts to help
his friend:

> My brother deere, I may do the no more. (1731)
> What sholde I seyn? I hate, ywys, Criseyde ...

But even now he cannot see the truth, as the ambiguity of
the last part of this final speech reveals:

> If I dide aught that myghte liken the, (1737)
> It is me lief; and of this tresoun now,
> God woot, that it a sorwe is unto me!
> And, dredeles, for hertes ese of yow,
> Right fayn I wolde amende it, wiste I how.
> And fro this world, almyghty god I preye,
> Delivere hire soone; I kan no more seye.

He still cannot connect: he is glad to have given Troilus
pleasure, and the only 'tresoun' that causes him sorrow is
Criseyde's.

CHAPTER V

Conclusion and Summary

IN the last chapter of *Seven Types of Ambiguity*, Empson writes:

... to say a thing in two parts is different in incalculable ways from saying it as a unit: ... When you are holding a variety of things in your mind, or using for a single matter a variety of intellectual machinery, the only way of applying all your criteria is to apply them simultaneously; the only way of forcing the reader to grasp your total meaning is to arrange that he can only feel satisfied if he is bearing all the elements in mind at the moment of conviction; the only way of not giving something heterogeneous is to give something which is at every point a compound.[1]

I can think of no better way to describe the function of the ambiguity in *Troilus and Criseyde*: to apply what he writes, in the way Empson does, to critical analysis is another matter. He had written, in the preceding paragraph, 'one wants as far as clarity will allow to say things in the form in which they will be remembered when properly digested'. But, alas, clarity rarely does allow, in the analysis of complex poetry. The problem for the analyst of *Troilus and Criseyde* is to convey his own apprehension of the 'compound' of its poetry, which comprises its emotional effect, its comedy, and wit, as well as its irony, and it is difficult to do full justice to all simultaneously, especially when a full understanding must depend in part on a recognition of

[1] pp. 238–9.

historical factors which may demand perhaps somewhat ponderous explanation. Yet some attempt must be made to convey exactly how all these factors work in the total effect of the poem—how the sympathy that the narrative invites is compatible with the irony, how the irony and the comedy are to be reconciled with the emotional effect of the poetry.

The most obvious emotional effect of the poetry is the fellow-feeling for the lovers that it seems to invite; and we might perhaps be tempted to reconcile this with the irony in terms of the natural tendency, in writer and reader alike, to take different attitudes to the behaviour of persons and to the persons themselves: our attitude to behaviour is generally governed by 'rational' considerations, whereas our attitude to people as persons is determined more by feeling—even to the extent that we tend to be drawn more to those who act from feeling themselves than from rational motives. But to explain the complex effect of *Troilus and Criseyde* in this way, I think, would be to falsify, to misrepresent the temper of the poet that has produced the particular form of expression. When he prays to Love in the Proem to the third book, 'Ye in my naked herte sentement | Inhielde, and do me shewe of thy swetenesse', he is using *sentement* in its double, medieval sense, to refer to both intellectual and emotional perception; and it is this kind of perception that informs the poem, determines its temper. It is by feeling this *sentement*, as well as by an understanding of his *sentence*, his message, that we perceive how the poet stands in relation to his subject. What may seem to be an incompatibility between the emotional effect of the poetry and its irony ceases to be so if the *sentement*, the intellectual and emotional perception, is such as to include the sympathy. The irony which serves to keep us in touch with the morality becomes perfectly compatible with the sympathy if the poet is seeing his subject through, not with, an ironic eye.

As an illustration of what the distinction may mean in our apprehension of the poem, I will take as my final passage for analysis Troilus' apostrophe to Criseyde's empty house, in the last book. I choose this passage because it is a 'poetic' passage, and therefore one in which the emotional effect must be reckoned with, while at the same time it contains ironic ambiguities which have moralistic implications. In this way it provides a good test of how the ambiguity may work in the total effect. For in the description of Troilus' reactions to Criseyde's depar⁄ture from Troy, which leads up to this passage, the reader's sympathy for Troilus has been steadily built up by im⁄plicit appeals to the fellow⁄feeling that anyone must have who has ever waited, alternating between hope and doubt, for something or someone desperately longed for. The only irony has been the dramatic irony, underlined at Troilus' moments of hope by interjections from Pandarus or the narrator. Yet Chaucer chooses the occasion of Troilus' visit to Criseyde's empty house, which he takes from Boccaccio, to bring a more ambiguous note into the depic⁄tion of Troilus' suffering. More than a week has gone by of the ten days' limit promised by Criseyde for her return, and Troilus goes with Pandarus, perhaps in the half⁄hope that she will have returned. For when he sees the doors all barred and the windows shuttered, he grows deadly pale and rides past quickly so that no one can see his face. And it is then that he speaks his apostrophe:

> O paleys desolat,   (v. 540)
> O hous of houses whilom best ihight,
> O paleys empty and disconsolat,

O thow lanterne of which queynt is the light,
O paleys, whilom day, that now art nyght,
Wel oughtestow to falle, and I to dye,
Syn she is went that wont was us to gye!

O paleis, whilom crowne of houses alle,
Enlumyned with sonne of alle blisse,
O ryng, fro which the ruby is out falle,
O cause of wo, that cause hast ben of lisse,
Yit, syn I may no bet, fayn wolde I kisse
Thi colde dores, dorste I for this route,
And farewel, shryne of which the seynt is oute.

When D. W. Robertson drew attention to the (possible)
pun on 'queynt' in the first stanza of this passage as 'bitter
comment on what it is that Troilus actually misses',[1] he
was putting an unfortunately simple view of what is far
from being a simple piece of writing. If there is a pun on
'queynt' its implications must be seen in the context of
the whole figure of the lantern and the light, and also in
relation to the other figures in the passage, as John F.
Adams has shown.[2] For the possibility of the pun on
'queynt' is not the only feature of these stanzas that may
make us suspect that there is more in them than may
appear on the surface. There is, to begin with, the use of
the term 'paleis' for Criseyde's house, which in the corre-
sponding passage in *Il Filostrato* is called simply 'la casa' or
'la magione'. The change, slight though it is, serves its
purpose in the transition from the earlier metaphors of
light (the lantern and the 'whilom day, that now art
nyght') to the astrological metaphor by which the light
becomes the 'sonne of alle blisse', which illuminated the

[1] 'Chaucerian Tragedy', pp. 34–5.
[2] 'Irony in Troilus' Apostrophe to the Vacant House of Criseyde', *MLQ*
xxiv (1963), pp. 61–5.

'paleis, whilom crowne of houses alle'. By this astrological metaphor the missing light becomes not only Criseyde herself, but what she represents to Troilus: as the sun, or planet, that is the source of *all* bliss, whose 'paleis' is the 'crowne of houses *alle*', the missing light becomes both Criseyde and Venus. But because the metaphors of light merge into each other in this way, each takes meaning from the other; and what first strikes an ironic note in the passage is the figure of the lantern and the light, since this was a figure that had become a commonplace to explain the nature of Christian chastity (from the parable of the virgins in Matthew 25).[1] As a Christian commonplace, the lamp is chastity and its light is charity: as Troilus uses the figure, the missing light becomes both Criseyde herself and what she represents for Troilus—the 'sonne of alle blisse'. So here we have the same kind of ironic ambiguity we have found so often earlier in the poem, where Christian imagery is adapted to the cult of Venus. If there is a pun on 'queynt' it must give an ironic inversion to the figure itself. The irony does not exactly depend on the pun, but the pun enriches the irony both by being a pun, and by underlining, more specifically, the inversion by which the lamp, that is chastity, becomes the 'paleis' both of Criseyde and Venus, and its light, that is charity, becomes 'queynt'.

It is possible also, though it would be difficult to prove, that the pun enriches the meaning in another way—if there is, in the 'light' metaphor in association with Venus, an oblique iconographical allusion. Adams draws attention to a painting on a fourteenth-century Italian tray, which depicts the naked body of Venus emitting rays of light, particularly the pudendum, from which six separate

---

[1] Adams cites *Piers Plowman*: 'Chastite withoute charite . . . is as lewed as a laumpe | That no liȝte is inne' (B i, 186–7).

beams go direct into the eyes of six kneeling knights,
named Achilles, Tristam, Lancelot, Samson, Paris, and
Troilus.[1] There is no evidence of course that Chaucer
knew this painting, but there is some supporting suggestion, besides the present passage, that he may have been
familiar with the concept of Venus (and Troilus) it
depicts, in a passage in the fourth book where Troilus goes
to his room to lament, after he has heard that Criseyde must
leave Troy. In his lament he apostrophizes his own eyes:

> O woful eyen two, syn youre disport   (IV. 309)
> Was al to sen Criseydes eyen brighte,
> What shal ye don but, for my discomfort,
> Stonden for naught, and wepen out youre sighte?
> Syn she is queynt, that wont was yow to lighte,
> In veyn fro this forth have ich eyen tweye
> Iformed, syn youre vertu is aweye.

If there is an ironic pun on 'queynt' in the apostrophe to
Criseyde's empty house, there must surely be one here too.
And if the pun is accepted we can see how purposeful and
interrelated these apostrophes of Troilus are. It is typical of
the irony of Chaucer's depiction of him that he expresses
what he is missing in terms which refer to Criseyde's
influence, or 'vertu', but which, by their ambiguity, in the
context, reveal the specific nature of that 'vertu'. (A
somewhat different example of the same method is the use
of the term 'conscience' in the portrait of the Prioress.)
In the earlier apostrophe Criseyde is identified with the
light that was wont to light Troilus' eyes—a light which is
'queynt'; in the apostrophe to Criseyde's house, she is both
the lantern's light—which is 'queynt', and the 'sonne of

---

[1] Reproduced in Roger S. Loomis and Laura H. Loomis, *Arthurian
Legends in Medieval Art* (New York, 1938), pl. 135, with explanatory text,
p. 70; and in J. A. W. Bennett, *The Parlement of Foules*, pl. 2*b*.

alle blisse' (Venus). It would be a remarkable coincidence
if there were no iconographical allusion. In the *Cantus
Troili*, which follows shortly after the address to Criseyde's
house, Troilus still sees what he is missing in astrological
terms, but here the ambiguity is more overt—perhaps because the point has already been made, more enigmatically:

> O sterre, of which I lost have al the light,   (638)
> With herte soore wel ought I to biwaille,
> That evere derk in torment, nyght by nyght,
> Toward my deth with wynd in steere I saille;
> For which the tenthe nyght, if that I faille
> The gydyng of thi bemes bright an houre,
> Mi ship and me Caribdis wol devoure.

There is another figure in the apostrophe to Criseyde's
house—'O ryng fro which the ruby is out falle'—which
has ironic implications leading back to the earlier part of
the poem, for this too is a figure that had been used before,
in the scene where Pandarus first tells Criseyde of Troilus'
love for her, and concludes thus:

> And right good thrifte, I prey to god, have ye,   (II. 582)
> That han swich oon ykaught withoute net;
> And be ye wis, as ye be fair to see,
> Wel in the rynge than is the ruby set.
> Ther were nevere two so wel ymet,
> Whan ye ben his al hool, as he is youre;
> Ther myghty god yit graunte us see that houre.

Here the surface meaning of the figure is the proverbial
comparison of wisdom with rubies, but in the whole context of Pandarus' words the figure must have a double
meaning: if Criseyde will be as wise as she is beautiful the
ruby will then be well set in the ring, in the same sense as
'Whan ye ben his al hool'. It is clear from the mention of

'that houre' how specific is the consummation Pandarus has in mind (a point Criseyde was quick to take), and if 'ryng' could have the sexual connotation it certainly has at a later date, we have another example of a pun adding to the ambiguity. In Troilus' address to Criseyde's house, the 'ryng fro which the ruby is out falle' must surely be complementary to the earlier 'Wel in the rynge than is the ruby set' and have a similar double meaning.[1]

How then are we to describe the total effect of Troilus' address to Criseyde's empty house? In what ways does the irony qualify the sympathy we have been made to feel for Troilus' suffering? It would be incongruous with the picture of him that we have been given to see the *double entendre* as intentional on his part; and it is a very Freudian view that would see it as unconscious self-betrayal. It is more a kind of dramatic ambiguity directed to the audience, methodologically similar to, yet different in effect from that of his address to the moon, later in the same book:

> For whan thyne hornes newe gynnen sprynge,   (657)
> Than shal she come, that may my blisse brynge.

In both addresses the irony is at Troilus' expense, but the difference is that the address to Criseyde's house invites a judgement from the reader. But is that all that it does? What the irony qualifies is Troilus' elevated language, which can describe in terms of empty palaces and extinguished lanterns and vacant shrines a loss which must have been felt in a much less abstract way, as the irony reveals (and as the *Cantus Troili* hints more openly). But

---

[1] Adams suggests that there may be a pun in the bedroom scene when Criseyde suggests sending a ring to Troilus to pacify him, and Pandarus replies: 'A ryng! . . . | Ye, haselwodes shaken . . .' (III. 890 ff.). There certainly seems to be some innuendo in Pandarus' reaction, but I think the passage I have quoted provides a closer parallel.

there is more to the ambiguity than the irony. Troilus' language, in his own meanings of the words, reflects his attitude: that he can see his loss in these elevated terms is itself a factor in the dramatic ambiguity. And though we may be amused at his unawareness of the possible double meaning of his words, and enjoy the poet's wit, our clearer vision does not inhibit the feeling we have for Troilus' suffering. Nor should it, in terms of the morality, if we see the point of the ambivalence. For 'to say a thing in two parts is different in incalculable ways from saying it as a unit': since it was the same blindness which prevented Troilus from recognizing the physical nature of the 'influence' he is missing that enabled him in all sincerity to describe his loss in these exalted terms, it is right that the same words that reveal what he is really missing should make us see his loss through his eyes. This is the most effective, and the most amusing way of bringing home to us the full nature of his blindness. It is not what he is really missing that is the point so much as the passion that can make him see his loss in these elevated terms—they are the measure of what his blind love has led him to, and correspondingly the measure of his suffering. To feel with him in his suffering, while at the same time realizing its real cause, is to apprehend both the measure of his passion and its nature.

This example serves to illustrate what is true in general of the ambiguity of the poem—that the sympathy and fellow-feeling for the persons in the story which the narrative invites is itself essential to our full apprehension of the morality that the irony serves to define. The 'allegory' is not simply saying one thing to mean another: it is allegory that works by providing a kind of living experience of what is allegorized, by involving the reader at all levels. At the most obvious level there are the many evocations of our pity for the lovers' suffering ('in this world ther nys so hard an herte | That nolde han rewed on hire peynes smerte'). But the irony ensures that our pity is not just the ready pity that suffering evokes: by opening our eyes to the nature of their love, it helps us to see the suffering as a consequence of the lovers' blindness, or 'sickness' of soul, and as such to be pitied in all charity. Even Pandarus' suffering at his inability to help Troilus is to be seen as a consequence of his own blindness in his earlier misguided efforts to help. But we must be involved also at a more emotional level if we are to understand fully the problem of love that the poem is putting to us. And it is here that the ambiguity of the narration becomes a way of presenting a story of love gone wrong in such a way that it encourages us to love. The medieval doctrine of love, which serves throughout as the touchstone for the irony, posited a 'natural law' of love by which sexual love can be comprehended in *caritas* in a harmonious relation, if the love is for the right reasons. This harmony was not achieved by the lovers in the story, as the irony is designed to reveal, and perhaps this is understandable, since they were pagans; but this negative point is not the main concern of the 'allegory'—it is only a way of making the positive, nonironical point that the harmony is 'natural', that sexual love can have its place in the divine order, or 'natural law' of love. The reader is reminded that sexual desire is a part of the 'lawe of kynde', and its power is stressed repeatedly, not only as a warning but as a fact of nature ('strengest folk ben therwith overcome, | The worthiest and grettest of degree'). And this positive point is made also, on a more emotional level, in the depiction of the love in the first part of the story. In one aspect (the ironical one), this can be seen as a depiction of the pro-cesses by which sexual desire can pervert love into an idolatrous passion, or into an unstable, worldly love, if the love is for the wrong reasons: in another aspect it is a depiction of the naturalness and power of sexual love itself. And it is in this latter aspect that the emotional involvement of the reader becomes important. A delicate balance is held between the emotion and the ironical detachment, as can be seen, for example, in the way that the roles of Pandarus and the narrator counterbalance one another in the bedroom scene: the presence of Pandarus, until he fades out of the picture, acts as a reminder of the 'game' that is being played, in contrast to the narrator's innocent enjoyment of the lovers' joy; but, paradoxically, it is Pandarus' 'bisynesse' that lends a kind of innocence to the lovers, while the ambiguities of the narrator's fervent interventions alert us to the dubiousness of the situation. The irony that distances us from the lovers, however, does not prevent us from emotional involvement in their joy, any more than it prevents us from involvement in their later suffering. The more clearly defined the moral boundaries the safer it becomes to venture into doubtful territory; and there is no inconsistency in our appreciation of the lovers' joy if we recognize that sexual pleasure has its place in nature's purpose. In the *Parlement of Foules*, Troilus is among the figures of tragic lovers (and perhaps by implication censured) painted on the walls of Venus' temple; but Venus has her place in Nature's garden. What the poet finds in his dream of that garden is an answer, or partial answer, to the problem of love that had perplexed him before he fell asleep—an answer which he had sought and not found in his 'olde bok':

> For bothe I hadde thyng which that I nolde,　　(90)
> And ek I nadde that thyng that I wolde.

What he had and did not want, from his reading, must surely be the contempt of this world which Africanus' words had advocated. Similarly, in *Troilus and Criseyde* the solution that is offered for the problem of love is not a contempt of this world, only a recognition that it 'nys bot a faire, . . . that passeth soone as floures faire'. The 'yonge, fresshe folkes, he or she', who are exhorted to recognize this, are those in whom 'love upgroweth with hire age'. Their love, like that of Troilus and Criseyde, will be prompted by the stirrings of sexual desire, and, like that of Troilus and Criseyde, it will be 'an entencioun to comen to good', a seeking for the perfect happiness. What the poet is encouraging these young people to do is, not to despise the happiness that sexual love can offer, but to be sure that the good their love is seeking is the real good. Only when we understand this does the real nature of Troilus' tragedy come home to us. The 'idealism' of his love which impresses the reader—especially in the great hymns to love in the third book—is not a sham: we need not deny it in recognizing the irony. The double response that the hymns evoke becomes the 'compound' of their meaning, if we realize that the Divine Love Troilus is praising is the Love his love was really seeking, and thought it had found. Those critics who find a 'triple scale of values' in the poem do so because, while they recognize that the love in the story must be distinguished from *caritas*, they feel that its 'idealism' or 'nobility' raises it above lust. But there is no triple scale of values: what makes possible the 'idealism' is the blindness of Troilus' passion, which elevates his physical love, in his own eyes, into a cosmic principle. But a sexual love that becomes an end in itself cannot be this. The 'parfit blisse' that Troilus' love was seeking could only be an illusory and mutable happiness when the love was for physical reasons—as the subsequent events of the story prove.

> Swich fyn hath, lo, this Troilus for love!
> Swich fyn hath al his grete worthynesse!

Because he was 'worthi', in the higher sense of the word, he deserves our sympathy. But his 'worthinesse' too suffers corruption in the blindness of his passion—to the extent that he can offer to procure for Pandarus his own sister. In this aspect he is an *exemplum* of the depths to which misdirected love can lead. But in another aspect, his 'idealism' and 'purity' and 'trouthe' make him an *exemplum* of the heights to which human love could rise if it were properly directed. It is this aspect that makes the narrative, for all its irony, an encouragement to love, and enables us to see that, in the ultimate analysis, the poet is seeing his subject through, not with, an ironic eye.

Criseyde's contribution to the 'allegory' of the poem complements that of Troilus, to round off the treatment of love, and evokes a similar double response. Where his love illustrates how the impulse to love, prompted by sexual attraction, can be deflected into an idolatrous passion, hers illustrates how the impulse to love, similarly prompted by sexual attraction, can be deflected by worldly and largely self-regarding considerations into the kind of love that is liable to change as circumstances change. Both are seeking the perfect happiness that is the objective of all love, but in their different kinds of blindness they take the wrong paths, because they love for the wrong reasons. Criseyde, like Troilus, sees her love idealistically—to the extent that she can tell Troilus in all sincerity, at their parting, that she loved him most for his moral virtue, and

that his reason bridled his 'delit', but such is the instability
of her kind of love that, later, she can reply to his letter
with the accusation:

> Nor other thyng nys in youre remembraunce,   (v. 1607)
> As thynketh me, but only youre plesaunce.

We can, with the poet, 'excuse hire yit for routhe', because
the ready pity, the 'ferfulnesse', and the 'tendre herte'
which have helped to motivate both her love and its
instability, are themselves traits which arouse our sympathy
for her. But what matters ultimately is the values that
determine the use of these qualities. Where Troilus
exemplifies 'trouthe' in love, albeit in a misguided service
of a 'false good', Criseyde, for all that she 'menes wel',
exemplifies, both as agent and victim, the 'slydynge corage'
inevitable in one whose values are the values of this
'slydynge' world.

Criseyde's function as an *exemplum* of one form that
'feyned love' (love for a wrong reason) can take, however,
is only a part of her whole function in the poem. She also
acts, as Pandarus does, to provide an unobtrusive commentary on the kind of love happiness the story illustrates—
in her references to the falsity of this world and the falsity of
worldly happiness. And her rebuke to Troilus for his
supposed jealous passion, in the third book, which has its
own irony as applied to the immediate situation, has a
deeper truth that applies to his love itself:

> And som so ful of furie is and despit,   (1037)
> That it sourmounteth his repressioun;
> But, herte myn, ye be nat in that plit,
> That thonke I god, for which youre passioun
> I wol nat calle it but illusioun,
> Of habundaunce of love and besy cure,
> That doth youre herte this disese endure.

The irony of the last part of this stanza lies, as the irony of this poem so often does, in the ambiguity of the word 'love': the 'illusioun' of Troilus' passion comes from the 'habundaunce' of his sexual desire and from his 'besy cure'—his preoccupation with the business of attaining his desire. In Augustinian terms such love is *cupiditas*, and in this aspect Chaucer is simply restating the Christian position. But his formulation of that position reflects the changing climate of thought which demanded a different language to express the position. What, for Boethius, could be comprehended simply under the heading 'delyces of body' becomes for Chaucer a problem of sexual love interesting and complex enough to justify the ambiguities by which he can use his story of an illicit love to demonstrate that 'every wight . . . |That loveth wel meneth but gentilesse'. This is the part of his message that evokes the strongest response in our newer climate of thought, so that it is easy now to overlook the questions he raises about what is to be understood by loving 'wel' and by 'gentilesse'. But even for those of us who cannot share the poet's Christian view of these questions there is another message in his story of the double sorrow of Troilus that is valid today—'Only connect'. Yet, for all that, if this essentially medieval work is to be paid the doubtful compliment of being dubbed 'modern', it should be for the sophistication of its use of language, its sheer skill with words: that it is modern also in the sense that what it has to say applies still in our age is a tribute to the medieval philosophy of love that informs it.

Appendix

Kynde and Unkynde[1]

WHEN C. S. Lewis distinguished five groups of meaning for
the adjective *kind*, he prefaced his list with the remark: 'It is not
possible to reconstruct the bridges between them, still less to be
sure in which direction the traffic crossed them'.[2] This applies
especially to the Middle English developments of the word, and
the following observations are intended only as a supplement
to Lewis's more comprehensive study of the whole complex of
meanings in which the adjective *kind* is used.

The semantic history of *kynde* and *unkynde* is fairly clear
up to a point: we can see how a word meaning 'natural' in the
sense of 'innate' or 'characteristic' (Anglo-Saxon *gecynde*) comes
to mean 'natural' in the sense of 'proper', 'appropriate'. As
Lewis observes, when Criseyde asks how any plant or living
creature can last without 'his kynde noriture' (IV. 768), 'it
is impossible to draw any distinction between an organism's
characteristic or normal, and its suitable or appropriate, food'.
Similarly, when her friends saw Criseyde weeping 'and
thoughte it kyndenesse' (IV. 720), the two meanings are closely
interrelated—'thought it only natural' and 'thought it proper,
appropriate, to her nature (or to woman's nature)'.

But when, after Criseyde's vows to be true to Troilus, we
are told that

> al this thyng was seyd of good entente;   (IV. 1416)
> And that hire herte trewe was and kynde
> Towardes hym . . .

[1] For a fuller, and more philosophical, treatment of the concept of 'kind' see
C. S. Lewis, *Studies in Words*, 2nd edn., C.U.P. 1967: Ch. 2, 'Nature',
pp. 26–33.
[2] *Studies in Words*, p. 27. For his discussion of the meanings of the adj.
kind see pp. 27–33.

what exactly is the meaning of *kynde*? It is easy enough to assume that it means exactly what it would mean now, and this would probably be Lewis's view: he regards the 'peculiar erotic use' of the adjective *kind* not as a special sense, but a special application of the sense he distinguishes as his fifth and last category, 'exorable, compassionate, beneficent—the opposite of cruel', the sense in which we use *kind* now. But it is not so certain from the evidence of medieval love poetry that *kind* always has this sense in its erotic use. *Kind* and *unkind*, applied to persons, can be used with various meanings in Middle English, most of which are listed by Lewis in his third and fourth categories: the adjectives can refer to nobility, loyalty, family feeling, generosity, gratitude. And as far as the medieval period is concerned there is no reason to dis-tinguish these uses or applications of the word from the uses or applications which come within Lewis's fifth category: we should not assume, because the meaning of *kind* has been narrowed in modern English to the meaning 'exorable, compassionate, beneficent—the opposite of cruel', that there was anything in the medieval use of the word to distinguish this application from, for example, the application to gratitude or loyalty.

The question is—what made it possible for *kynde* to be used in Middle English with such various meanings? And the answer may well lie in the fact that the word still retained at that period its earlier, etymological, senses, 'innate', 'natural', 'characteristic', and the related senses, 'proper', 'appropriate'. In the Harley Lyric called *The Poet's Repentance*, in the line 'Cunde comely ase a knyght' (65), *cunde* has its etymological meaning (as in *gecynde*), 'having a specified character by nature or birth', specified here by 'comely'. But in the lyric *God, þat Al þis Myghtes May*, in the line 'ne to my kunde Louerd drawe' (26), *kunde* is used absolutely, but in a context that identifies 'natural' or 'proper', by implication, with 'good' or 'kind' in the modern sense. Similarly when Langland writes: 'Ne on croked kene þorne kynde fygys wexe' (*Piers Plowman*,

C iii, 29), he is identifying the goodness of the figs with their nature, just as Trevisa is identifying the unnatural with the bad or *unkind*, in the modern sense, when he writes: 'þe lenger he lyueþ þe more he scheweþ þat his owen kynde is unkynde'.[1]

While *kynde* and *unkynde* still had in Middle English this basic reference to what is 'natural' or 'proper' they became words that lent themselves easily to different colourings in different contexts by assuming reference to whatever quality or attitude is natural or proper to the particular situation. Thus *unkynde* can mean 'undutiful', or 'lacking in filial feeling'— 'Vn⁻kynd i was . . . Gayn fader and moder' (*Cursor Mundi*, 28270); or 'unnaturally cruel'—'Unkynde kiþe ʒe ʒou to kille ʒour children' (*Alexander and Dindimus*, 540); and un⁻ *kyndenesse* can mean 'niggardliness'—'Diues deyed dampned for his vnkyndenesse | Of his mete and his moneye to men þat it neded' (*Piers Plowman*, B xvii, 263). In all these examples the reference is to the lack of the feeling 'natural' or 'proper' to the situation, and it seems reasonable to assume that when *kynde* and *unkynde* are used in the meaning closest to the modern meaning there is a similar reference implied.

Lewis remarks that *kind* often has 'a vaguely eulogistic sense', and cites as one example 'kind jeweler' in *Pearl* (276). But if we look at the *Pearl* passage it will be seen that the sense of *kynde* there is by no means vague. The passage is a part of the Pearl's speech, rebuking her father for his rebellious grief when he should be rejoicing at her heavenly state.

> Bot, jueler gente, if þou schal lose   (265)
> þy ioy for a gemme þat þe watʒ lef,
> Me þynk þe put in a mad porpose,
> And busyeʒ þe aboute a raysoun bref;
> For þat þou lesteʒ watʒ bot a rose
> þat flowred and fayled as kynde hyt gef.
> Now þurʒ kynde of þe kyste þat hyt con close

---

[1] Cited in *OED*, s.v. Unkind, sense 3 d.

To a perle of prys hit is put in pref.
And þou hatȝ called þy wyrde a þef,
þat oȝt of noȝt hatȝ mad þe cler;
þou blameȝ þe bote of þy meschef,
þou art no kynde jueler.

I have quoted this stanza in full because it seems to illustrate so well what was happening to the adjective *kynde* in Middle English, especially in the fourteenth century. In one sense, *kynde*, as applied to the father, implies here 'grateful'—the quality or attitude proper to the situation: instead of railing against the fate that robbed him of his transitory 'rose' the father should be grateful that it has become a 'perle'. And this application of the adjective *kynde* must have been a well-established one, since Lydgate in *The Fall of Princes*, writing about ingratitude, can describe it as this vice called *unkyndnesse*, and Elyot similarly can refer to ingratitude, commonly called *unkindnesse*. But, applied to the jeweler in the *Pearl* stanza, *kynde* also has something of the connotation that associates the adjective with the noun *kynde*, used twice earlier in the stanza; he is no proper or 'born' jeweler who does not recognize, or put the true value on, the 'perle of prys'.

Thus when Langland writes: 'iche cristene man be kynde to oþer | And siþen hem to helpe' (*Piers Plowman* A xi, 243), can we be sure he means by *kynde* exactly what we should mean now, as Lewis suggests when he cites this example in his fifth category? Is there not also, inherent in the word, a stronger association than we might suppose with the idea of what is 'natural' or 'proper'—in this case proper to Christian men in relation to their fellows? In medieval literature *kynde* and *unkynde*, applied to persons, usually refer to personal relations, and the common factor, and the one that links them with the other uses of *kynde*, seems to be that they refer to what would be 'natural', 'proper', or 'appropriate' in the particular situation. And this may help to explain the 'peculiar erotic use' of the adjectives. They refer to the presence or absence of the quality or attitude proper to the situation, and though

this is most often the 'beneficent or exorable' attitude, it is not
always so. In the Proem to the fourth book of *Troilus and
Criseyde*, the narrator tells us:

> For how Criseyde Troilus forsook,   (15)
> Or at the leeste how that she was unkynde,
> Moot hennesforth ben matere of my book.

Chaucer does not seem to be using *unkynde* here in the sense in
which we use it now. He uses *kynde* and *unkynde* repeatedly in
the last two books in contexts which suggest that he means not
so much *kind* and *unkind* in the modern sense as 'true' and 'un-
true' or 'loyal' and 'disloyal':

(Troilus to Criseyde)

>   certes, if ye be unkynde,   (IV. 1440)
> And but ye come at day set into Troye,
> Ne shal I nevere have hele, honour, ne joye.

(Criseyde to Troilus)

> For in this world ther lyveth lady non,   (IV. 1646)
> If that ye were untrewe, as god defende,
> That so bitraised were or wo-bigon
> As I, that alle trouthe in yow entende.
> And, douteles, if that ich other wende,
> I nere but dede; and or ye cause fynde,
> For goddes love, so beth me naught unkynde.

(Diomede to Criseyde)

> But wolde nevere god but if as trewe   (v. 124)
> A Grek ye sholde among us alle fynde
> As any Troian is, and ek as kynde.

(Troilus, as he abandons hope of Criseyde's return)

> He ne eet, ne dronk, ne slep, ne no word seyde,   (v. 1440)
> Ymagynyng ay that she was unkynde.

It seems probable, as Lewis suggests, that in the use of *kind*
to describe a woman who yields to her lover's suit 'euphemism
and gallantry, not always without a touch of irony' have played
a part. But so also may a consciousness of the other meanings

of *kynde*: an exorable attitude to a deserving lover is 'natural' and 'proper'. But as the passages just quoted seem to demonstrate this is not the only meaning of *kynde* in the love situation. It is also proper in the courtly ideal to be constant in love: anyone who violates the ideal of constancy is *unkynde*, in the same way that ingratitude is *unkyndenesse*.

It is in the medieval usages that the seeds of the modern development of the adjective *kind* lie. By the end of the fourteenth century the most frequent uses, as applied to persons, are to qualities of character or behaviour that involve relations between persons. *Kynde* implies a proper, that is a good, human quality or attitude, but it cannot be used of *any* good human quality—not, for example, of bravery, endurance, honesty, or any qualities except those that are immediately relevant to personal relations. And it is not perhaps too fanciful to suggest that the gradual limitation to the modern meaning was helped in its direction by association with the related noun *Kynde*. The concept of nature comprehended in the word *Kynde* was deeply embedded in medieval thought, through the influence of sermons and love poetry, and sermons especially had a strong influence on the language. Since it is *Kynde* that determines a man's attitude to his fellows and to God, it is not surprising that the adjective *kynde* comes to have a special reference to that attitude. When we use the phrase 'take kindly to' a person, we are using *kindly* with the same double connotation it has in *Pearl*, when the father implores his daughter in heaven, 'kyþeȝ me kyndely your coumforde' (369)—the kindliness is natural feeling as well as benevolence.

LIST OF REFERENCES TO
TROILUS AND CRISEYDE

INDEX

Adams, John F., 133-4, 137 n.
Alain de Lille, 25: *De Planctu Naturae*, 67.
Alexander and Dindimus, 147.
Andreas Capellanus: *De Amore*, 38.
St. Augustine (of Hippo), 6, 7, 144.

Bacon (Francis): *Of the Wisdom of the Ancients*, 16, 17, 19, 22.
Bennett, J. A. W., 68 n., 135 n.
Benoit de Sainte Maure: *Roman de Troie*, Briseida, 110, 111 n.
Bethurum, Dorothy, 52 n., 53.
Boccaccio: *Il Filostrato*, 19, 31, 42, 60, 62, 63-4, 66, 70, 77, 82, 83, 88, 90, 106, 107, 110, 111 n., 117, 118, 122, 124, 126, 132, 133; Troilo, 31, 32, 33, 64, 78, 82, 107, 110, 117, 122, 123; Griseida, 82, 83, 101, 105, 107, 109, 110; Pandaro, 125.
Boethius: *Consolation of Philosophy*, 19, 22, 23, chap. II *passim*, 61, 69, 72, 73, 93, 100, 125, 144; Philosophia Chap. II *passim*, 69.
Borthwick, Sister Mary Charlotte, 98 n.
Brewer, D. S., 52 n., 68 n.

Chaucer: *Canterbury Tales*, Prol., Monk, 8-9, Prioress, 85, 135, *Knight's Tale*, 73 n., *Squire's Tale*, 54 n., Wife of Bath's Prol., 27, *Monk's Tale*, 67 n.; *Nun's Priest's Tale*, 45; *Parlement of Foules*, 68, 69 n., 72-3, 79, 97, 120, 140-1; Prol. to *Legend of Good Women*, 33; *Truth*, 53 n.

Curry, W. C., 47, 48-9.
Cursor Mundi, 147.

Dante, 19: *Paradiso*, 37.
Donaldson, E. Talbot, 13, 57.
Dunlap, Rhodes, 16.

Elyot, 148.
Empson, William: *Seven Types of Ambiguity*, 1-2, 7, 10, 130.

Fowler, H. W., 9.
French romance, 18, 39, 82, 113: Dame de Fayel, 82; *Eneas*, Lavinia, 81; Fénice, 82; Lydaine, 82; Ydoine, 82; *Yvain*, Laudine, 91, 126.

Gaylord, Alan T., 56 n., 84 n., 108 n., 115, 123.
Gilson, Étienne, 48 n.
Gower, 54.
Guido delle Colonne, 111 n.
Guillaume de Lorris, 121.
Guillaume de Machaut: *Paradis d'Amour*, 98.

Harley Lyrics, 146.

James, Henry, 10.
Jean de Meun, 25, 67, 91, 121.
Jefferson, B. L., 30 n., 33 n.

Kaske, R. E., 5-6.
Kean, P. M., 21, 63-5, 66.
Kittredge, G. L., 98 n.